Assisting Children with Additional Needs in ELC

Eilis Flood and Aisling Kirby

BORU

PRESS

Boru Press Ltd.

The Farmyard

Birdhill

Co. Tipperary

www.borupress.ie

© Eilis Flood and Aisling Kirby 2021

ISBN 978-1-8384134-8-4

Design by Sarah McCoy

Print origination by Liz White Designs

Illustrations by Andriy Yankovskyy

Index by Eileen O'Neill

Printed by Printer Trento srl., Italy

A CIP catalogue record for this book is available from the British Library. For permission to reproduce photographs and artworks, the author and publisher gratefully acknowledge the following:

© Alamy: 10, 41, 51, 57, 59, 61, 90, 114, 126, 129, 131, 136, 140, 156, 171, 172, 181, 183, 192. © Department of Childhood, Equality, Disability, Integration & Youth: 102, 106, 107, 109, 215, 216. © Down Syndrome Ireland: 191. © Dreamstime: 58, 128. © Eilis Flood: 65. © Guy's and St. Thomas' NHS Foundation: 59, 128. © iStock: 47, 102, 126, 127. © Mary Immaculate College: 85. © Safefood: 143. © Shutterstock: 5, 11, 21, 24, 28, 44, 60, 77, 81, 115, 116, 122, 125, 126, 127, 128, 129, 130, 142, 159, 167, 170, 173, 175, 179, 180, 183, 185, 186, 187, 190, 195, 196, 198, 206, 213.

The author and publisher have made every effort to trace all copyright holders, but if any has been inadvertently overlooked we would be pleased to make the necessary arrangement at the first opportunity.

Boru Press is an independent publisher and is not associated with any education and training board.

Contents

Preface

This book is written for learners completing the QQI Level 5 award in Early Learning and Care. Learners must have access to their professional placement in order to facilitate work-based learning.

KEY FEATURES

* Each chapter begins with an **I will learn** explainer, which outlines the learning in the chapter.

* Intertwined with the theory are practical teaching and learning strategies that support deep learning opportunities:

  > **Collaborate:** These sections ask learners to collaborate with peers to complete learning tasks. These tasks have been designed to be completed in person or online using a synchronous or asynchronous approach. Students and teachers are invited to be creative in their approaches to the Collaborate sections, adapting them as they see fit to their class style and demographic.

  > **Extend Your Learning:** These sections promote self-directed learning. Each occurrence will suggest you either look at a relevant website, complete online research or read a relevant publication; each research method will be indicated by the icons below:

  > **Reflective Practice:** These sections ask the learner to link a new learning experience to their professional placement context.

  > **Case Study:** These sections link theoretical knowledge to practical applications.

* Each chapter concludes with a **Show you know** section, which gives a brief summary of what the chapter contained and asks a series of questions inviting the learner to 'check your knowledge'.

Acknowledgements

I wish to express my deepest appreciation to everyone, both professional and personal, who contributed to the writing of this book.

To Marion O'Brien, publishing director, Anna Carroll for managing the production of this book, copy editor Paula Elmore, designer Liz White and proofreader Caitriona Clarke. Thank you for all your hard work and attention to detail.

To Aisling Kirby, co-writer on this book, who took on this project with such professionalism, creativity and care.

Finally, on a personal level, thanks to Paddy, Luke and Mark for your continuous support and encouragement.

Eilis Flood, 2021

I would like to thank my family and work colleagues, particularly Catherine O'Sullivan who provided continuous support in the writing of this book. To all the students who I had the privilege to work with over the years, thank you for sharing your experiences. To the families of children with additional needs with whom I worked during my time with Enable Ireland; the insight you gave me into your wonderful lives inspired me while writing this book.

Lastly to Eilis and Marion, thank you for your support and encouragement along the way.

Aisling Kirby, 2021

Section 1

Additional Needs of Children in Early Learning and Care

Additional Needs Concepts, Definitions and Terminology

1.1 INTRODUCTION

As an Early Learning and Care Practitioner (ELC) it is always important that you use the correct language to describe children with additional needs and understand the key concepts, definitions and terminology associated with working with children in your care with additional needs. In this chapter the following key concepts, terms and definitions shall be explored:

∗ Congenital

∗ Genetic and Inherited

∗ Acquired

∗ Developmental

∗ Progressive

∗ Hidden

∗ Environmental

1.2 CONGENITAL

Additional needs are said to be **congenital** when they are present from birth. Additional needs that are congenital may be caused by several factors, e.g. genetic factors or issues that arise during pregnancy or during labour and childbirth. Examples of congenital additional needs caused by genetic factors include Down syndrome and some forms of hearing and visual impairment. Examples of congenital additional needs caused by issues arising during pregnancy are spina bifida and foetal alcohol syndrome. Examples of congenital additional needs caused by complications during labour and childbirth are cerebral palsy and hydrocephalus.

1.3 GENETIC AND INHERITED

Many conditions that cause children to have additional needs have a genetic element and are therefore inherited from one or both parents.

Genetics is the scientific study of heredity and hereditary variation. **Genes** are the basic units of genetics. Human beings have approximately 20,000–25,000 genes. Genes are made up of strands of DNA (deoxyribonucleic acid). Genes (made up of DNA) are packed into **chromosomes** in each cell of the body. All body cells, except for the ova (eggs) and sperm cells, contain 23 pairs of chromosomes – one set of 23 from the mother and one set of 23 from the father.

How genes function is best described by using our understanding of written language. Just as your brain translates the word 'banana' into the mental image of a long yellow fruit, cells translate genes into characteristics such as blue eyes, curly hair or freckles. In addition, certain conditions and syndromes are also transmitted genetically that can pose mild to severe challenges for children's development and result in the child having additional needs.

1.4 ACQUIRED

Acquired additional needs refer to conditions that occur after birth and are not caused by hereditary or developmental factors but by environmental factors. Acquired additional needs can be caused by:

* Accident-related injuries: head trauma, spinal injuries, loss of vision, loss of hearing, injury to/ loss of limbs.

* Illness and health related: Infections such as meningitis, measles and rubella can cause conditions such as hearing impairment; post-traumatic stress can be caused by childhood abuse or neglect; mental illness such as anxiety can also be caused by abuse or neglect.

* Home environment: Some children can have additional needs as a result of a poor home environment. Children who have little experience of being read to, being spoken to or being given stimulating activities to participate in can experience challenges in ELC settings and later in school.

1.5 DEVELOPMENTAL

All additional needs impact on one or more areas of development. Some impact on only one area of development whereas others impact on two or more. Chapters 3–7 of this book detail a range of additional needs impacting on children's development.

* Chapter 3 will focus on additional needs primarily impacting on physical development, e.g. spina bifida.

* Chapter 4 will focus on additional needs primarily impacting on cognitive or intellectual development, e.g. general learning disability.

* Chapter 5 will focus on additional needs primarily impacting on the development of language and communication, e.g. hearing impairment.

* Chapter 6 will focus on additional needs primarily impacting on emotional and social development, e.g. Attention Deficit and Hyperactivity Disorder (ADHD).

* Chapter 7 will focus on complex additional needs impacting on more than one area of development, e.g. Down syndrome.

1.6 PROGRESSIVE

Most additional needs are not progressive, meaning they do not get more severe as time goes on. In fact, with timely and effective intervention, children with non-progressive additional needs can progress developmentally, reaching their full potential. A smaller number of additional needs are progressive, i.e. the condition becomes more severe as the child gets older despite interventions. One example of such an additional need is Duchenne muscular dystrophy (DMD). DMD is characterised by progressive weakening and wasting of the external and internal muscles of the body, eventually causing severe health issues and physical disability.

1.7 HIDDEN

Significant numbers of children with additional needs do not have their additional need diagnosed and as a result do not receive the interventions and supports that they require to reach their full potential, e.g. many children with dyslexia develop strategies to cover up their additional need for many years. When this occurs the additional needs is said to be hidden.

CASE STUDY

Ellen was not diagnosed with dyslexia until recently. She comes from a very academic family, all of whom have succeeded effortlessly in school and later in university. She always knew she had difficulty with reading and spelling but was somehow able to cope until the heavy workload of the Leaving Certificate came upon her. All through her schooling until that point she managed very well, achieving high grades. She has a very high IQ and found understanding the content of what she was learning up until that stage very easy. →

That meant that she was able to spend her time focusing on how to write down the information so that she could understand it. It was not until the content became challenging that she encountered great difficulty. She began to experience severe anxiety and found that she could not cope with the workload. Ellen dropped out of school after Christmas in fifth year and did not return. When Ellen was 26 years old, she decided to enrol

in a pre-arts course in a Post-Leaving Certificate college. One day she asked the career guidance and counselling teacher if she could speak to her. During the first session Ellen disclosed to the counsellor that she thought she had dyslexia. The counsellor was very supportive and arranged for Ellen to have a dyslexia screen and assessment done. Ellen was actually relieved when her dyslexia was confirmed. She received a spelling and grammar waiver for all her assessments and achieved eight distinctions. Her high grades allowed her to earn a place on a Level 8 veterinary nursing degree programme through the DARE (Disability Access Route to Education) scheme.

1.8 ENVIRONMENTAL

As you saw in section 1.3 above, many conditions that result in children having additional needs are as a result of genetics or heredity. Some conditions, however, are caused by the environment experienced by the child or mother either before conception, during pregnancy or after birth. These conditions are also related to 1.4 above, i.e. acquired additional needs. For a detailed description of these environmental factors that can result in children having additional needs, please see chapter 2.

SHOW YOU KNOW

Choose three of the following concepts, definitions and terminologies related to children with additional needs and write a note on each one:

* Congenital
* Genetic and Inherited
* Acquired
* Developmental
* Progressive
* Hidden
* Environmental

Factors that May Lead to Children Having Additional Needs

What I will learn

* The factors that may occur prenatally and can lead to a child having additional needs.
* How problems arising during labour and childbirth may lead to a child having additional needs.
* How issues arising postnatally may lead to a child having additional needs.

2.1 INTRODUCTION

There are many factors that may lead to a child having additional needs. Sometimes these factors are genetic and occur at conception; others occur as a result of factors during pregnancy, labour and childbirth. A small number occur as a result of accidents, illness or injury after birth and during childhood. This chapter shall first look at prenatal factors, then factors occurring during childbirth and labour, and finally at postnatal factors.

2.2 PRENATAL FACTORS

GENETIC

As you saw in chapter 1, many conditions that cause children to have additional needs have a genetic element and are therefore inherited from one or both parents and are present from conception.

In general, when we speak about genetic inheritance causing additional needs there are three main categories.

1. Single-gene inheritance

2. Complex multifactorial inheritance, also called polygenic inheritance

3. Chromosomal inheritance

Single-gene inheritance: Single-gene inheritance occurs when abnormalities occur in the DNA sequence of a single gene. There are thousands of known single-gene disorders and syndromes, which cause varying degrees of challenge and additional need for the individual. The following additional needs are classified as single-gene inheritance:

* Cystic fibrosis (see chapter 3)

* Duchenne muscular dystrophy (see chapter 3)

* Hearing impairment (see chapter 5)

* Marfan syndrome

* Phenylketonuria

* Sickle cell anaemia (see chapter 3)

Complex multifactorial inheritance, also called polygenic inheritance: Complex multifactorial gene inheritance disorders are sometimes called polygenic inheritance disorders. These occur when more than one factor causes a trait or health problem. The main factor is genetic, but the cause can include many other factors such as nutrition, lifestyle, alcohol or tobacco consumption, some medicines, illness and pollution. Due to the genetic component of many of these conditions and the shared environment over many generations, these conditions tend to run in families. This, of course, is not always the case; these conditions are complex and multifactorial and therefore identifying and exact 'cause' is frequently not possible. Conditions that have a genetic element and may also be in part caused by the other factors listed above include:

* Asperger's syndrome (see chapter 6)

* Asthma (see chapter 3)

* Attention Deficit and Hyperactivity Disorder (ADHD) (see chapter 6)

* Autism (see chapter 7)

* Cleft lip and/or palate

* Dyscalculia (see chapter 4)

* Dysgraphia (see chapter 3)

* Dyslexia (see chapter 5)

* Dyspraxia (see chapter 3)

* Epilepsy (see chapter 3)

* General learning disability (see chapter 4)

* Neural tube defects, e.g. spina bifida (see chapter 3)

* Psoriasis

* Specific speech and language impairment (see chapter 5)

* Type 1 diabetes (see chapter 3)

* Visual impairment (see chapter 3)

Chromosomal inheritance: As you learned in chapter 1, all an individual's body cells, except for the ova (eggs) and sperm cells, contain 23 pairs of chromosomes – one set of 23 from the mother and one set of 23 from the father. Chromosomal disorders can either be numerical or structural. When a numerical disorder occurs, the individual has either an extra or is missing a full chromosome. On the other hand, when a structural disorder occurs, only part of the chromosome is missing or duplicated. Additional needs caused by numerical disorders include Down syndrome (see chapter 7), Klinefelter's syndrome, XYY syndrome and Turner syndrome.

PRECONCEPTION HEALTH

Preconception health is a woman's and her partner's health before they become pregnant. It means knowing how health conditions and risk factors can affect their unborn baby in the event of a pregnancy. For example, some foods, habits and medicines can harm an unborn baby, even before they are conceived. Some health problems, such as diabetes, also can affect pregnancy.

Health Considerations for Women Before Pregnancy:

1. Take 400 to 800 micrograms (400 to 800 mcg or 0.4 to 0.8 mg) of folic acid every day to lower the risk of some birth defects of the brain and spine, including spina bifida.

2. Stop smoking and drinking alcohol.

3. Ensure that medical conditions such as asthma, diabetes, oral health, obesity or epilepsy are under control.

4. Talk to your doctor about any over-the-counter or prescription medicines you are using. These include dietary or herbal supplements. Ensure vaccinations, especially rubella, are up to date.

5. Avoid contact with toxic substances or materials that could cause infection at work and at home. Stay away from chemicals and cat or rodent faeces.

Health Considerations for Men Before Pregnancy:

1. Men and women should make the decision about pregnancy together. When both partners intend a pregnancy, the woman is more likely to get early prenatal care and avoid risky behaviours such as smoking and drinking alcohol.

2. Screening for and treating sexually transmitted infections (STIs) can help make sure infections are not passed on to female partners and subsequently their baby.

3. Male partners can improve their own reproductive health and overall health by limiting alcohol, quitting smoking or illegal drug use, making healthy food choices and reducing stress.

4. Men who work with chemicals or other toxins should be careful not to expose their partners to them. For example, people who work with fertilisers or pesticides should change out of dirty clothes before contact with their partner. They should handle and wash soiled clothes separately.

HEALTH DURING PREGNANCY

Teratology is the name given to the study of the causes of birth defects and resulting additional needs. A teratogen is anything that can potentially cause a birth defect or negatively affect any area of the child's development. Teratogens include drugs, infectious diseases, advanced maternal or paternal age, environmental pollutants, incompatible blood types and nutritional deficiencies.

Exposure to teratogens during the very early stages of pregnancy (0–2 weeks, called the germinal period) will normally prevent implantation, so pregnancy will frequently not occur. If the pregnancy does continue, teratogens generally have the most damaging effects if exposure occurs during the embryonic stage (weeks 2–8 after conception). This is when organogenesis occurs (formation of vital organs) and therefore structural damage to the organs may occur. Exposure during the foetal stage (weeks 8–40) normally causes stunted growth and problems with organ function.

1. EXPOSURE TO DRUGS

Prescription and non-prescription drugs: Prescription drugs such as the antibiotic streptomycin, found to cause deafness, and Accutane (isotretinoin), a drug given to treat acne and which has been found to cause brain, heart and facial defects, should be completely avoided during pregnancy. Non-prescription drugs that can be harmful include slimming tablets and aspirin. To be safe, women who suspect they may be pregnant should not take any form of medication without first consulting their doctor.

Extend your learning

Thalidomide is a drug that was developed in the 1950s by the West German pharmaceutical company Grünenthal. It was originally intended as a sedative or tranquilliser but was soon used for treating a wide range of other conditions, including colds, flu, nausea and morning sickness in pregnant women. During early testing, researchers at the company found that it was virtually impossible to give test animals a lethal dose of the drug. Based on this, the drug was deemed to be harmless to humans. Thalidomide was licensed in July 1956 for over-the-counter sale in Germany. During the 1950s, 14 pharmaceutical companies were producing and marketing thalidomide and selling it in 46 different countries under at least 37 different trade names. At that time, scientists did not know that the effects of a drug could be passed

through the placental barrier and harm a foetus in the womb, so the use of medications during pregnancy was not strictly controlled. And in the case of thalidomide, no tests were done involving pregnant women, with devastating effects. It is estimated that over 10,000 babies worldwide were affected by the drug. It was withdrawn in the 1960s.

One very harsh lesson that the thalidomide cases taught the pharmaceutical industry is that drugs intended for human use could no longer be approved purely on the basis of animal testing. Drug trials for substances marketed to pregnant women also had to provide evidence that they were safe for use in pregnancy. (Consider the debate around the vaccination of pregnant women with Covid-19 vaccines.)

Psychoactive drugs: Psychoactive drugs are drugs that act on the nervous system, causing changes to the individual's physical and mental state. Examples of psychoactive drugs include caffeine, alcohol, nicotine, marijuana, cocaine and heroin.

* **Caffeine:** Caffeine is found in tea, coffee, chocolate, cola and other soft drinks, e.g. Red Bull. Studies have found that caffeine intakes in excess of 200 milligrams (two cups of tea or coffee) increase the risk of miscarriage and low birth weight. Pregnant women should therefore avoid caffeine or consume very little.

* **Alcohol:** Alcohol consumption during pregnancy can have devastating effects on the child. Foetal alcohol spectrum disorders (FASDs), sometimes referred to as foetal alcohol syndrome (FAS), are a cluster of abnormalities and problems that appear in the offspring of mothers

who drink alcohol during pregnancy. Effects of the condition vary from child to child but include:

* Facial abnormalities such as wide-set eyes, thin upper lip, flat cheekbones and unevenly paired ears.

* Heart defects.

* Limb defects, particularly of the right hand and forearm.

* Learning problems – many have below-average IQ and a significant number have severe learning difficulties.

* Impaired memory functioning.

* Increased incidence of attention deficit and hyperactivity disorder (ADHD).

* The children will be prone to addiction themselves.

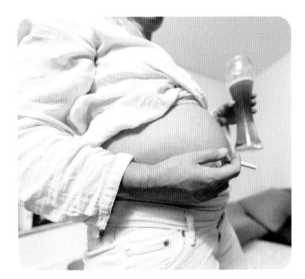

* They will also be prone to depression and other psychiatric illnesses later in life.

* A large proportion grow up to become unemployed, with many unable to live independently (Spohr, Williams and Steinhausen, 2007).

* **Nicotine:** Smoking cigarettes during pregnancy increases the risk of the baby being preterm and having low birth weight, of respiratory problems, and of foetal death and sudden infant death syndrome (SIDS). Studies also link smoking during pregnancy with increased irritability, lower scores on cognitive tests and increased inattention in children (Van Meurs, 1999). Others argue that such differences could be due to other environmental factors as well as smoking. Women who quit smoking during early pregnancy can avoid these problems, thereby reducing the risk to their baby to that of the level of a non-smoker.

* **Marijuana:** There have been several longitudinal studies carried out into the effects of marijuana use during pregnancy. Effects include reduced intelligence, memory and information-processing skills as well as increased childhood depression and early marijuana use by the child themselves (Fried and Smith, 2001). Marijuana should not be used in pregnancy.

* **Cocaine:** Cocaine use during pregnancy can cause a myriad of negative effects in children, such as low birth weight, reduced head circumference, prematurity, higher excitability and irritability, slower motor development, slower growth rate, increased risk of ADHD and learning difficulties and impaired language development. Some researchers recommend that these results be viewed with caution, as it is also more likely that mothers who use cocaine also live in poverty, are badly nourished and use other harmful substances such as alcohol, nicotine, marijuana and other drugs.

Extend your learning

'Charities working with drug users have expressed concern around the number of people presenting with crack cocaine dependency.' (RTÉ, 11 June 2021)

Crack cocaine is highly addictive. It is derived from powdered cocaine by combining it with water and another substance, usually baking soda (sodium bicarbonate). During pregnancy the use of crack cocaine is highly dangerous and can result in:

- Placental abruption, when the placenta separates from the uterus, potentially resulting in heavy bleeding or even death of the baby and the mother.
- Premature birth (earlier than 37 weeks).
- Low birth weight (less than 5 lb 8 oz).
- Miscarriage, or loss of the baby before 20 weeks.
- Neonatal abstinence syndrome (NAS), when babies are born addicted to a drug and experience withdrawal after birth.

* **Heroin:** Babies born to heroin users and users of the heroin substitute methadone are likely to experience withdrawal symptoms such as tremors, poor sleep patterns, irritability and shrill crying. 'Heroin babies' are more likely to have ADHD and experience behavioural problems as they get older. There is also the possibility of HIV infection being passed on as a result of using dirty needles.

2. BLOOD INCOMPATIBILITY

Everyone is born with a specific blood type and Rhesus (Rh) factor. The four different blood groups are A, B, AB and O, and the Rhesus factor is either Rh-negative or Rh-positive. Most people are Rh-positive, with approximately 15% of white people Rh-negative (Rh-negative blood is much less common among black and Asian populations, at approximately 5%). Blood incompatibility can arise if the mother is Rh-negative and her baby is Rh-positive. This is because the mother's body may begin to produce anti-Rh-positive antibodies that can pass across the placenta and harm the baby. This does not usually happen on the first pregnancy, but if the baby and mother's blood mix during labour and birth (which they are likely to do), the mother may then begin producing anti-Rh-positive antibodies that pass across the placenta and harm any subsequent Rh-positive baby.

Straight after birth, a sample of blood from the baby's umbilical cord will be tested to determine whether the baby is Rh-positive or negative. In addition, a sample of the mother's blood will be taken to determine the number of foetal blood cells present in her own blood. If foetal cells are found and the baby is Rh-positive, then the mother will be given an anti-D injection that will prevent her from developing anti-Rh-positive antibodies which could harm subsequent Rh-positive babies.

If anti-D was not given, serious complications would arise – babies could be born with severe life-threatening anaemia, liver damage, hearing loss or learning disability. They could also suffer seizures, cardiac failure and even death.

3. MATERNAL DISEASES AND INFECTIONS

Certain maternal diseases and infections can cause defects and complications in the newborn, either because they pass across the placenta to the foetus during pregnancy or are transmitted to the baby during the birthing process.

* **Rubella (German measles)**, while a mild disease for the pregnant woman, causes prenatal and neonatal (just after birth) deafness, blindness, learning difficulties, heart defects and death. In Ireland in the past, many pregnant women contracted rubella and had babies who either died or were severely affected by the condition. Since 1971, the rubella vaccine has been administered to pre-pubertal girls, and to both boys and girls since 1988. Currently, the MMR (measles, mumps and rubella) vaccine is offered at 12 months with a booster at four to five years to all babies born in Ireland. Unfortunately, in part as a result of a much-criticised paper linking the MMR vaccine and autism, vaccine uptake for MMR dropped to 80%, thus putting the population again at risk of rubella (Deer, 2009). Women who are thinking of becoming pregnant should have a blood test to confirm their immunity to the disease.

* **Diabetes** occurring in non-diabetic women during pregnancy is called gestational diabetes. It occurs in approximately 4% of pregnancies, but women who are obese are much more likely to develop it. Usually if women monitor their diet and take regular exercise, gestational diabetes does not pose problems. Sometimes, however, pre-eclampsia occurs, where the mother's blood pressure rises to unacceptable levels and protein appears in the urine. Babies of women who have badly controlled diabetes mellitus type 1 and 2 (meaning they have diabetes even when not pregnant) are at an increased risk of birth defects and prematurity.

* **Pre-eclampsia** is when women experience high blood pressure during pregnancy. It is commonest in women who have had it in previous pregnancies, older women, obese women and women carrying twins or more. If blood pressure becomes unacceptably high, the baby will be delivered early either by induction or Caesarean section, as failure to do so could cause serious brain damage in the child.

* **HIV/AIDS**: AIDS is a life-threatening infection (usually sexually transmitted) caused by the human immunodeficiency virus (HIV). A mother can infect her baby with HIV in several different ways: during pregnancy across the placenta, during birth through contact with maternal blood or fluids, or through breastfeeding. However, transmission rates from mother to baby can be reduced to approximately 2% if antiviral drugs are given during pregnancy, the baby is delivered by Caesarean section and is not breastfed. If babies are born HIV positive, their average life expectancy is very low (three years) in countries where they are left untreated. Recent improvements in treatments available in the developed world mean that children born with HIV will live longer, but average life expectancy is still only ten years. Since the introduction of the antenatal HIV screening programme in Ireland in 1999, mother-to-child transmission of HIV has been dramatically reduced. Of the total of 106 babies born to HIV-infected mothers in 2008, only two were diagnosed with HIV infection, and one of these was born to a mother who was not known to be infected during pregnancy and who later tested positive.

* **Genital herpes simplex** is an incurable sexually transmitted infection caused by the herpes simplex virus (HSV). There are two distinct types of HSV. Type 2 is most commonly associated with genital infection. Type 1 has also been found to cause genital infection but is more commonly associated with oral herpes (cold sores). Most infected individuals experience mild symptoms or none. If present, symptoms include one or more blisters at the site of infection and a burning sensation during urination. After the initial infection, HSV remains dormant in the body for life and may reactivate from time to time. If a baby passes through the birth canal of a woman with an active case of genital herpes, then the risk to the baby is high – they may suffer brain damage or die. Therefore, a Caesarean is normally performed in these cases.

* **Syphilis** is a serious sexually transmitted infection caused by the bacterium Treponema pallidum. If it goes untreated, it can have serious effects on all the organs of the body. Unlike rubella, which damages organs during organogenesis (production and development of the organs), syphilis attacks organs after they have formed, causing blindness, learning delay, seizures and even death.

4. OTHER FACTORS

Other factors that may affect prenatal development are maternal age, maternal diet and maternal stress, as well as paternal factors.

Maternal age: When considering maternal age and foetal development, two age groups are significant: adolescence, and women aged over 35.

Did you know?

According to figures from the Central Statistics Office (CSO), the number of teenage mothers who gave birth decreased by 60.2% during the ten years between 2008 and 2018, with 956 teenage mothers giving birth in 2018, compared to 2,402 in 2008.

Pregnant adolescents younger than 17 years have a higher incidence of medical complications involving mother and child than do adult women, although these risks are greatest for the youngest teenagers. The incidence of having a low birth weight infant (weighing less than 2,500 grams) among adolescents is more than double the rate for adults, and the neonatal death rate (within 28 days of birth) is almost three times higher. The mortality rate for the mother, although low, is twice that for adult pregnant women. Why is this? Several factors are believed to be involved:

* Immature reproductive system.

* Low pre-pregnancy weight and height.

* Poor nutrition.

* Low socioeconomic status resulting in poverty.

* Low education levels and lower rates of engagement with prenatal care.

* Higher rates of sexually transmitted infections.

* Substance misuse (cigarettes, alcohol and other drugs).

Women of 'advanced maternal age', previously called 'geriatric mothers', are those having their first child at 35 years or older. Advanced maternal age, particularly when combined with other factors such as obesity and poor maternal general health, can lead to several potential issues:

* Greater risk of general maternal health problems, such as high blood pressure and gestational diabetes.

* Higher risk of miscarriage.

* Higher risk of having twins or triplets.

* Increased risk of having a baby with a congenital abnormality, e.g. Down syndrome.

* Increased risk of complications during delivery, such as prolonged labour, need for assisted delivery, Caesarean section or stillbirth.

Did you know?

The numbers of women in Ireland giving birth for the first time over the age of 35 has steadily increased in recent years. According the CSO (2017), Ireland has the highest average age of first-time maternity (32.8 years) of any EU country.

Maternal diet: A balanced diet is essential during pregnancy for the baby's general health. Obese women can pose a risk to their developing baby – there is an increased risk of prenatal death, gestational diabetes and pre-eclampsia. Recent studies of children whose mothers gained excessive weight during pregnancy have shown that they are more prone to childhood and adolescent obesity themselves. Folic acid is also important for the prevention of neural tube defects and should be taken in tablet form to supplement dietary sources such as citrus fruits.

Maternal stress: When a pregnant woman experiences intense stress, there is an increase in the stress hormone cortisol, both in her blood and in the amniotic fluid surrounding her unborn baby. Cortisol has been found to pass from amniotic fluid to babies of highly stressed women. The main cause of stress in pregnant women is relationship problems. While some studies (Glover *et al.*, 2005) link stress during pregnancy with premature delivery, lower IQ and anxiety and attention problems in children, others believe that these effects merely reflect the environment the baby is born into or the effect of stressed mothers using alcohol or other drugs to cope with stress.

Paternal factors: There are several paternal factors that are thought to adversely affect foetal development.

* Exposure to radiation, lead, mercury, cocaine and certain pesticides can cause sperm abnormalities, leading to increased rates of miscarriage and childhood cancer.

* A diet low in vitamin C in fathers can also result in increased rates of birth defects and cancer.

* Fathers who smoke during and after their partner's pregnancy may have children of low birth weight. Later, if the father continues to smoke, babies are at an increased risk of sudden infant death syndrome and childhood cancers.

* Fathers of advanced age (40+) are also more likely to have children with birth defects, although the link between birth defects and maternal age is much stronger.

2.3 FACTORS OCCURRING DURING LABOUR AND CHILDBIRTH

Premature birth is a birth that takes place more than three weeks before the baby's estimated due date. In other words, a premature birth is one that occurs before the start of the 37th week of pregnancy. Premature babies, especially those born very early, can have complicated medical problems. Depending on how early a baby is born, they may be:

* **Late preterm,** born between 34 and 36 completed weeks of pregnancy

* **Moderately preterm,** born between 32 and 34 weeks of pregnancy

* **Very preterm,** born at less than 32 weeks of pregnancy

* **Extremely preterm,** born at or before 25 weeks of pregnancy

In the early weeks after birth many premature babies experience short-term complications that are treated in special-care baby units. In the longer term, premature birth may lead to several complications such as cerebral palsy, learning disabilities, vision problems, hearing problems, social and emotional problems and chronic health conditions.

The vast number of pregnancies and births occur with no serious issues. However, there are several rare childbirth complications that can occur causing oxygen deprivation to the baby and subsequent brain injury.

Uterine rupture is a very rare and serious event in which the wall or lining of the mother's uterus tears open. The rupture of the uterine wall occurs suddenly and usually without any warning. When this occurs, the baby is under immediate threat of oxygen deprivation, which causes brain damage or even death. When a uterine rupture occurs, the baby must be delivered by Caesarean section within 10–30 minutes.

Shoulder dystocia is an emergency event that can occur suddenly during a vaginal delivery. It occurs when the baby's shoulder becomes stuck while entering the birth canal, usually on the mother's pelvic bone. Shoulder dystocia requires doctors to act quickly to dislodge the baby to avoid oxygen deprivation and the subsequent risk of brain injury and the development of additional needs such as cerebral palsy.

Umbilical cord prolapse, when the umbilical cord drops down into the cervical opening in front of the baby as it enters the birth canal, occurs very rarely. It is very serious because as the baby's head pushes down, it will compress the cord against the pelvis restricting or even completely cutting off the baby's oxygen supply.

Chorioamnionitis is a complication that occurs during pregnancy whereby a maternal bacterial infection travels up to the uterus and infects the amniotic fluid and foetal membranes. This type of infection, if not detected and treated (usually by delivering the baby), can cause oxygen deprivation and brain injury.

Foetal macrosomia is the scientific term for a baby that is too large for safe vaginal delivery. If a baby becomes stuck in the birth canal during delivery, there is a risk of oxygen deprivation, which can result in brain injuries.

2.4 POSTNATAL FACTORS

Most additional needs occur due to genetic causation, prenatal or birth events. Postnatal causes account for far fewer cases.

Bacterial meningitis, which accounts for the largest number of cases, causes an inflammation or swelling of the membranes that surround and protect the brain and spinal cord. It is a very dangerous infection and can often be fatal. Some bacteria that cause meningitis can also cause septicaemia or blood poisoning. Children who have had bacterial meningitis may experience long-term problems, such as epilepsy, brain damage, hearing and sight loss.

Did you know?

Below are listed the common signs of meningitis and septicaemia in babies and toddlers. Not all symptoms may be present. Parents and those caring for young children are always advised to err on the side of caution and seek medical assistance immediately if meningitis is suspected.

- Convulsions/seizures
- Drowsiness, floppiness, unresponsiveness
- Fever, cold hands and feet
- Fretful, dislike of being handled
- Pale blotchy skin or a rash
- Rapid breathing or grunting
- Refusing food and vomiting
- Stiff neck, dislike of bright lights
- Tense bulging fontanelle (soft spot on head)
- Unusual cry or moaning

Child abuse: Non-accidental head injury is the leading cause of death and long-term disability among babies who are abused. It is also called abusive head trauma (AHT) and was previously called 'shaken baby syndrome'. It is estimated that there is one case per month in Ireland of non-accidental head injury in babies (Nicholson, 2016).

Accidents: Near-drowning incidents, falls and motor-vehicle crashes can also cause serious injury that results in children acquiring disabilities.

Chronic disease: Children can have heart disease or cancer resulting in strokes and brain tumours that can have a long-term impact on their development.

SHOW YOU KNOW

1. Describe **three** factors that may occur prenatally and can lead to a child having additional needs.

2. Explain **three** problems that can occur during labour and childbirth that may lead to a child having additional needs.

3. Describe **three** issues that can occur postnatally that may lead to a child having additional needs.

Additional Needs Affecting Physical Development

What I will learn

* Understand a range of additional needs that affect physical development.

3.1 INTRODUCTION

This chapter introduces additional needs that can impact on children's physical health and development. It explores how these additional needs can impact on a child's life and how effective ELC settings can support children's learning and development in these settings. The additional needs that will be addressed in this chapter (in alphabetical order) are:

* Asthma
* Cerebral Palsy
* Cystic Fibrosis
* Developmental Dyspraxia
* Diabetes mellitus
* Dysgraphia
* Epilepsy
* Hydrocephalus
* Muscular Dystrophy
* Sickle Cell Disease
* Spina Bifida
* Vision Impairment

3.2 ASTHMA

PREVALENCE

Ireland has the fourth-highest rate of asthma in the world (behind Australia, New Zealand and the UK) (HSE, 2021). According to the Irish Asthma Society, one in every ten children have asthma with one in five having asthma at some stage during childhood. It is therefore very likely as an ELC practitioner that you will have children in your care with asthma.

REFLECTIVE PRACTICE

Why do you think diagnosed asthma rates are much higher in developed countries such as Australia, New Zealand, the UK and Ireland than in less developed countries such as Vietnam (where the rate is 1%)?

CAUSES

The causes of asthma are not fully understood. An individual can develop asthma at any time in life, although it most commonly begins in childhood. Genetics are thought to play a role – it often runs in families – but it can occur with no family history. Individuals with other conditions, such as hay fever, eczema or other allergy-type complaints, are more prone to asthma. In short, however, the reasons why asthma rates are increasing worldwide are not known.

Extend your learning

The 'hygiene hypothesis' was put forward in 1989 by British epidemiologist David Strachan and in the same year by German epidemiologist Erika von Mutius. Strachan found that children from large, crowded families tended to have lower rates of hay fever and eczema than children from smaller families. He believed that increased exposure to pathogens from their many siblings protected children in large families from allergies. Von Mutius was researching the effect of air pollution on asthma in what was then East and West Germany. She was shocked to find that children from dirtier, more polluted East Germany had dramatically less asthma than their West German counterparts, who were living in cleaner, more modern circumstances. The East German children, unlike their Western counterparts, had spent more time in day care and thus had probably been exposed to many more viruses and bacteria. Both believed that early childhood exposure to bacteria and viruses caused children's antibodies to become more active, thus keeping the allergy and parasite-related cells in check.

In groups, discuss the 'hygiene hypothesis' in relation to dramatically increasing rates of asthma among children in Ireland over the past 30 years.

SYMPTOMS OR CHARACTERISTICS

The commonest symptoms of asthma are listed below. They may be brought on by exercise, changes in air temperature or irritants in the air, e.g. pollen, dust or animal hair. Colds or chest infections can bring on attacks or worsen symptoms.

* Coughing, particularly at night

* Difficulty breathing/shortness of breath

* Feeling of tightness in the chest

* Hoarseness

* Wheezing

TREATMENT AND SUPPORTS

The main treatment for asthma is medication. Preventers, controllers, relievers and steroids are all terms that children with asthma are familiar with.

* **Preventers/controllers:** These are inhalers that help prevent the swelling and inflammation of the airways. This helps the airways to become less sensitive to irritants and reduces the risk of attacks. The effect of preventers/controllers builds up over time, so they need to be taken every day, usually once in the morning and once in the evening. It is important that the child with asthma takes or is given their preventer/controller even when they are well, as this is what is keeping them well. Preventer inhalers usually contain a low dose of steroid, which reduces inflammation. For some children, preventers/controllers alone are not sufficient, and a combination inhaler may be prescribed. This inhaler will contain a steroid plus a long-acting reliever (see below).

* **Relievers:** Everyone with asthma will have a reliever. Relievers are taken immediately when the symptoms of asthma occur. Relievers work by quickly relaxing the muscles around the airways, allowing them to widen and helping the child to breathe more easily. They do not reduce swelling and inflammation, like preventers/controllers do. If relievers are taken before activity, they reduce the chances of an attack. Relievers normally come in a blue inhaler. Examples include salbutamol (e.g. Ventolin) and terbutaline (e.g. Bricanyl). Children should not have to use relievers too often (more than once or twice a week); if being used more frequently than this, it indicates that their asthma is not well controlled.

* **Steroids:** If a child's asthma gets particularly bad, a short course of steroids may be prescribed, usually over the course of three to 14 days.

ROLE OF THE ELC PRACTITIONER

Preventer/controller medication is normally taken in the mornings and evenings, so it will not usually have to be taken by the child while in the ELC setting. Make sure the setting has a full history of the child's asthma and that all staff members are familiar with the child's known triggers, their medications and what to do in the event of an attack.

If a child is having an asthma attack:

1. Stay calm yourself.

2. Immediately give them their reliever inhaler (usually blue) and have them take two puffs.

3. Sit the child upright and help them remain calm.

4. Tell them to take slow, steady breaths.

5. If there is no immediate improvement, it is usual for the child to take another puff once every minute (up to ten puffs in ten minutes) until symptoms improve. For children under six years of age, it is usually up to six puffs in six minutes.

6. If symptoms do not improve, call an ambulance. Repeat steps 1 to 4 until it arrives.

It is important not to let the child lie down and not to put your arm around him/her, as this further restricts breathing. Do not restrict the use of their reliever: during an attack, extra puffs of reliever are safe. Listen to what the child is saying: they are likely to have had attacks before and know what they are talking about. With younger children, a spacer is often used to administer reliever.

Spacer being used to administer reliever in a young child

3.3 CEREBRAL PALSY

Cerebral palsy (CP) is an umbrella term used to refer to a group of complicated conditions that affect movement and posture because of damage to or failure in the development of the part of the brain that controls movement. The severity of the condition depends on the area of the brain that has been damaged and the extent of that damage. Severity can range from children having few mobility difficulties to having severe mobility difficulties whereby the child will need assistance with all areas of mobility, i.e. sitting, feeding, toileting.

PREVALENCE

Based on 59,796 births per annum (CSO, 2019), with a CP incidence rate of 1.77 per 1,000 births, it is estimated approximately 110 children are born annually with cerebral palsy in Ireland.

CAUSES

Cerebral palsy occurs when the brain fails to develop normally or is damaged either before, during or shortly after birth.

Before birth:

* Infections, particularly rubella, toxoplasmosis (an infection that comes from parasites found in animal faeces or undercooked meat) or other viral infections.
* Failure of the placenta to develop and function effectively.
* Use of some drugs during pregnancy, e.g. cocaine.
* 'Vanishing twin' – some cases of cerebral palsy are thought to be caused by the death of an identical twin sharing the same placenta. The death of one twin is thought to cause a disruption in the flow of blood to the surviving twin.

Around birth:

* A prolonged, difficult labour where the baby's brain is deprived of oxygen.
* Prematurity – between 40 and 50% of babies born with cerebral palsy are premature.
* Infections.
* Multiple births.

After birth:

* Physical brain injuries – falls, abusive head trauma (previously called 'shaken baby syndrome').
* Infections such as meningitis, encephalitis, severe jaundice.
* Hypoxia (oxygen deficiency to the brain) caused by near drowning, choking or poisoning.
* Brain tumours.

SYMPTOMS AND CHARACTERISTICS

There are three main types of cerebral palsy, each of which will have different symptoms or characteristics and can vary in severity:

* Spastic cerebral palsy
* Dyskinetic cerebral palsy
* Ataxic cerebral palsy

Spastic cerebral palsy is the most widely known and commonest form of CP, affecting up to 60% of all children with this additional need. Damage occurs to the motor cortex, located in the outer layer of the brain. This area of the brain manages thought, movement and sensation. This causes an abnormally strong and sometimes painful tension in the muscles of the arms and legs. If the person tries to move a joint, the muscles contract and block or stop the movement. Arms are often held at an angle. The child's fist may be clenched. The child may have what is called scissoring, where the legs come inwards at the knees with toes pointed outwards. The term 'spastic', while a medical term, should never be used to describe someone with CP, as it is hurtful and offensive.

Dyskinetic (or athetoid) cerebral palsy is less common, thought to affect 20 to 25% of children with CP. It results from damage to the basal ganglia, which are located in the middle of the brain, below the cortex. The basal ganglia are involved with coordinating and controlling the movement of the muscle groups. All limbs may or may not be involved. Movement will be jerky and irregular, and the child will normally make twisting movements with their fingers and wrists. If the legs are affected, then the child will walk in a lurching manner with uncoordinated arm movements. Emotional stress may make the condition worse. A baby with athetoid CP, unlike a baby with spastic CP, will be floppy, slow to gain head control and to sit.

Did you know?

There are three different forms of dyskinesia CP: dystonia, athetosis and chorea. Each of these results from injury to slightly different structures within the basal ganglia.

Ataxic cerebral palsy is the rarest form of CP, affecting between 1 and 10% of children with CP. It results from damage to the cerebellum, which is the area of the brain concerned with balance. A child with ataxic CP will have difficulty balancing and will sometimes walk with a high stepping motion on tiptoe. The child may also have difficulty typing, writing or using scissors. Nystagmus (rapid eye movement) is often present with this type of CP.

Children with CP are also described in terms of how many limbs are affected by the condition.

 * Quadriplegia: This is most the most severe form of CP – all four limbs are affected.
 * Hemiplegia: One side of the body is affected.
 * Paraplegia: Only the legs are affected.

ASSOCIATED CONDITIONS

Some children may have a combination of all three types and many also have other additional needs (Johnson, 2002):

 * General learning disability (IQ < 50): 31%
 * Moderate to severe general learning disability: 20%
 * Epilepsy: 21%
 * Visual impairment: 11%
 * Wheelchair use: approximately 20%

TREATMENT AND SUPPORTS

The treatments and supports offered to children with CP will vary in accordance with the type of CP they have and with how severe it is. Treatments include:

- ✳ Medications to lessen muscle tightness and manage pain, e.g. Botox.
- ✳ Physical therapy to improve muscle strength, balance and mobility and to use adaptive equipment such as walkers and wheelchairs.
- ✳ Occupational therapy to help children gain independence in daily living skills.
- ✳ Speech and language therapy to help children to speak more clearly, use sign language or use communication devices and to address issues with eating and swallowing.
- ✳ Some children require surgery to lessen muscle tightness or correct bone abnormalities.

ROLE OF THE ELC PRACTITIONER

The level of assistance required by the child will depend on the severity of their condition. A system called the gross motor function classification system is used to categorise different levels of mobility for children with CP. The classification system has five levels.

Level 1: Babies and young children will be slightly later reaching milestones but may be able to walk without assistance by their second birthday and by their sixth birthday will be beginning to run and jump. Speed, balance and coordination will be somewhat limited. ELC practitioners should present plenty of opportunities for children to practise emerging physical skills.

Level 2: Babies and young children will be significantly slower reaching milestones, e.g. at age two they will still use hands for balance in the sitting position. Children between two and four may prefer to crawl on hands and knees, or cruise holding onto furniture or walk with an assistive mobility device such as a walker. ELC practitioners will need to assist children moving around the room or outside space safely.

Level 3: Infants (0–2 years) will need continuous back support while sitting but may be able to roll and push themselves along while lying on their tummy. ELC practitioners should provide safe spaces for infants to do this. Crawling is generally the preferred method of moving around (2–4 years), while children (4–6 years) may be able to push themselves to stand by holding onto something sturdy and walk for short distances using a walker. Again, ELC practitioners should provide plenty of opportunity for the child to practise their emerging physical skills.

Level 4: Infants (0–2 years) will need assistance to sit up. Children (2–4 years) may be able to sit up alone but will use hands for balance. At this level, children use crawling as their preferred method of moving around. By age six children may be able to walk short distances using a walker but should always be monitored because of issues with balance and coordination.

Level 5: Infants (0–2 years) will require assistance holding their head up. Children (2–6 years) will require assistance in all areas of movement. ELC practitioners should ensure that children are involved in as many activities as possible.

3.4 CYSTIC FIBROSIS

Cystic fibrosis (CF) is a genetically inherited condition that causes one or more of the glands of the body to produce a thick, sticky mucus that affects organ function. The commonest organs affected by CF are the lungs and the organs of the digestive tract, especially the pancreas (which is also part of the endocrine system).

PREVALENCE

Cystic fibrosis is Ireland's commonest life-threatening inherited disease. Ireland has the highest incidence of CF in the world, with more than 1,300 children in Ireland living with CF.

CAUSES

Cystic fibrosis is caused by mutations in a gene called gene CFTR on chromosome 7. CFTR is a gene that provides instructions for making a protein called the cystic fibrosis transmembrane conductance regulator. Through the process of osmosis, this protein regulates the movement of water in and out of the mucus membranes of many of the organs, particularly the lungs, digestive system, liver, pancreas and reproductive organs. When the CFTR gene is faulty, the mucus becomes overly thick, causing the organs to clog and malfunction. CFTR also regulates salt loss from the body via the sweat glands. Patients with CF usually secrete large amounts of salt in their sweat (before the availability of genetic testing, this was how CF was diagnosed). As the gene CFTR is recessive, for someone to have CF, both their parents must either be carriers of the defective gene or have the condition itself.

SYMPTOMS

* Very salty-tasting skin.

* Persistent coughing, at times with phlegm.

* Wheezing or shortness of breath.

* Frequent greasy, bulky stools or difficulty in bowel movements.

* Poor growth and weight gain despite a good appetite.

TREATMENT AND SUPPORT

Treatment and support for children with CF generally centre around five different areas:

* Maintenance of good nutrition.

* Prevention of infection, particularly lung infections.

* Physiotherapy to keep the airways clear.

* Organ transplants.

* New medications.

Did you know?

On 28 April 2021 the European Commission granted approval of the drug Kaftrio® for most (over 80% of) people aged over 12 with CF in Ireland. This is the first drug manufactured to treat the underlying causes of CF.

ROLE OF THE ELC PRACTITIONER

An ELC practitioner working with a child with CF will agree with the child's parents/guardians what additional supports the child requires. In general, however, an ELC practitioner may have the following roles:

* Carrying out physiotherapy sessions with the child, several times a day if necessary.

* Making sure the child is eating their lunch and has taken their enzyme supplement.

* Administering other medication, e.g. antibiotics or inhalers as required.

* Ensuring that children cough into tissues and dispose of them safely.

* Helping children with good personal hygiene to prevent the spread of infection.

* Helping to keep the child's environment clean and well ventilated.

* Ensuring that other children do not come into the setting when they are unwell as children with CF can become very ill if they pick up infections.

3.5 DEVELOPMENTAL DYSPRAXIA

Developmental Coordination Disorder (DCD), also known simply as dyspraxia in Ireland and the UK, affects fine and/or gross motor skills coordination.

PREVALENCE

Dyspraxia is a relatively common disorder affecting up to 6% of children with a ratio of 3:1 among boys and girls (Dyspraxia Ireland, 2021).

CAUSES

It is not clear why dyspraxia or DCD occurs in some children although several risk factors can increase a child's likelihood of developing DCD.

* Being born prematurely.

* Being born with a low birth weight.

* Having a family history of DCD, although it is not clear exactly which genes may be involved.

* Mother drinking alcohol or taking illegal drugs during pregnancy.

SYMPTOMS OR CHARACTERISTICS

Children under six will generally not be yet diagnosed with dyspraxia but some of the following indicators may be present in younger children:

* May be slow to reach developmental milestones, e.g. sitting up and crawling.

* Poor balance – may frequently fall over.

* Difficulty throwing or catching a ball.

* Poor awareness of body position in space, e.g. frequently bumps into things.

* Poor sense of direction.

* Difficulty hopping, skipping or pedalling a tricycle or bike.

* Sensitive to touch, e.g. dislikes the 'feel' of certain clothing.

* Confused about right and left.

* Intolerant of having hair/teeth brushed, or nails/hair cut.

* Slow to learn self-care skills, e.g. dressing or feeding.

* Difficulty with pre-writing skills, e.g. learning to hold a pencil properly, using a scissors, etc.

* Slow learning to speak.

* May have phobias, obsessive behaviours and be impatient.

* Disorganisation.

* Difficulty staying still for any length of time.

SUPPORTS FOR CHILDREN WITH DYSPRAXIA

While there is no cure for dyspraxia, there are several options available to help the child improve their skills and deal with the emotional and social effects of having the condition. Depending on the characteristics of their dyspraxia, children will often work with a combination of occupational therapist, physiotherapist and speech and language therapist. Children with dyspraxia are often not able to correctly position what are called the speech articulators (face, tongue, lips and jaw) and may have difficulty pronouncing sounds, syllables and words. With two or more years of intensive speech therapy, most children will eventually be capable of communicating very well. If the child has poorly developed gross motor skills, e.g. running, jumping, throwing, catching or kicking a ball, or riding a bicycle, they may begin working on balance and coordination skills with a physiotherapist, who can build up the child's muscle strength and tone and increase awareness of their limbs. For children experiencing problems with their fine motor skills, e.g. handwriting, tying laces or putting on clothing, an occupational therapist can concentrate on the child's coordination, using skills such as threading, cutting, colouring and copying shapes and patterns.

ROLE OF THE ELC PRACTITIONER

Allow the child plenty of time to process new tasks, offering plenty of praise and encouragement. Present daily routines and tasks in a step-by-step way and be very patient. Provide a visual demonstration of tasks rather than just verbal instruction. Give the child plenty of opportunity to practise the new skills they have learned, e.g. putting on their coat or tying their laces. Sometimes children with dyspraxia have difficulty planning what they want to do themselves, e.g. they may be at the Lego box and wish to build a house. Help them with the task by scaffolding or supporting them with their planning. Teach the child ways to ask for help, e.g. 'Can you show me?' or 'How should I do that?'

3.6 DIABETES MELLITUS

There are two main categories of diabetes: type 1 and type 2. Type 1 diabetes tends to occur in childhood or early adult life and always requires treatment with insulin injections. It is caused by the body's own immune system destroying the insulin-making cells (beta cells) of the pancreas. When the body cannot produce insulin, it is unable to regulate blood sugar levels in the body.

PREVALENCE

It is estimated that approximately 2,000 Irish children have diabetes. Most of these children have type 1, but an increasing number of obese older children and young adults are developing type 2.

CAUSES

Diabetes mellitus is a lifelong condition caused by a lack of, or insufficiency of, insulin. Insulin is a vitally important hormone made by the pancreas. Insulin acts like a key to open the doors into body cells, letting sugar (glucose) in. With diabetes, the pancreas makes too little insulin to enable all the sugar in the blood to get into the muscle and other cells of the body to produce energy. If sugar cannot get into the cells to be used, it builds up in the bloodstream. Diabetes is therefore characterised by high blood sugar levels. Type 1 diabetes is classified as a polygenic disease, meaning it is caused by several different genes. Type 1 diabetes can be caused by both genetic factors and environmental triggers. Some environmental triggers thought to increase the likelihood of diabetes are prenatal rubella infection, high birth weight, older maternal age and low intake of vitamin D during pregnancy. Postnatal triggers are thought to include some infections and weaning babies too early.

SYMPTOMS

The four main symptoms of type 1 diabetes are:

* **Thirst:** Excess drinking, unable to quench thirst.
* **Toilet:** Frequent urination, particularly at night.
* **Tiredness:** Lack of energy, sleeping more than usual.
* **Weight loss:** Rapid weight loss over a short period.

TREATMENT

Currently, diabetes cannot be cured but it can be treated. Diet and insulin therapy are the two main ways to control it. Generally, the person (or their carer) monitors their blood sugar levels at intervals throughout the day (the skin is pricked, a small amount of blood taken and tested in a blood glucose monitor). The person (or their carer) then administers insulin by way of a subcutaneous injection. Children are usually taught to do this from a relatively early age. Some children may be fitted with a continuous glucose monitor and an insulin pump. Continuous glucose monitors measure glucose levels through tiny sensors inserted under the skin; the information is displayed on a small monitor or on a mobile phone app. Insulin pumps are small computerised devices that are programmed to deliver a certain amount of insulin throughout the day. At certain times they also deliver a 'bolus' quantity of insulin for after meals.

In terms of diet, people with type 1 diabetes generally avoid foods high in refined sugars, e.g. cakes, sweets, in favour of foods that release energy more slowly. Individuals with type 1 diabetes must eat regular meals and snacks.

ROLE OF THE ELC PRACTITIONER

It is quite rare for a child under the age of six to be diagnosed with diabetes. However, increasingly younger children are being diagnosed with the condition. Should a child with diabetes be enrolled in an ELC setting, specific training for setting staff is essential. When this training is complete, the role of the ELC practitioner is to monitor the child's blood sugar levels, ensure that they eat regular meals and snacks and administer their insulin injections at the prescribed times. In addition, ELC practitioners need to be able to recognise the signs of a hypoglycaemic attack (low blood sugar) at its earliest stages and know what to do. It is important that practitioners stay calm and do not frighten the child or other children in the setting.

Did you know?

The symptoms of hypoglycaemia (low blood sugar) are shakiness, dizziness, sweating, pale skin and sleepiness.

If a child is showing signs of hypoglycaemia, they need to consume an easily absorbed form of sugar, e.g. sugar lumps, granulated sugar or milk (usually 200 ml). If necessary, the child should be given more within ten minutes in addition to food with a slower energy release, e.g. bread.

If a child has difficulty controlling diabetes, those caring for the child may be given a special injection containing glucagon for use in emergencies. This injection would be given if the child was beginning to lose consciousness or perhaps was having a seizure due to low blood sugar levels. If this occurs in an ELC setting, it is a medical emergency and an ambulance should be called immediately.

3.7 DYSGRAPHIA

Dysgraphia is a learning disability that primarily affects the child's fine motor skills. Usually dysgraphia is not diagnosed until the child is in school and demonstrates a difficulty with handwriting.

PREVALENCE

It is estimated that approximately 6% of children have dysgraphia. It is much more common in boys.

CAUSES

Dysgraphia tends to run in families, so there is thought to be a genetic link. In some cases, dysgraphia can also be caused by brain injury during birth, childhood or even adulthood or as part of another condition, particularly ADHD and autistic spectrum disorders.

SYMPTOMS OR CHARACTERISTICS

Frequently, children will not be diagnosed with dysgraphia until they are in school and are required to handwrite. In the ELC setting, the following may indicate that a child could have dysgraphia:

* Resists colouring or drawing.
* Holds crayons or markers awkwardly.
* Often complains that drawing hurts or makes their hand tired.
* Struggles with activities such as join-the-dots, tracing or other writing activities that require patterns to be followed.
* May have difficulty picking up small objects.
* Struggles to copy letters.
* Rarely chooses colouring or drawing activities during free play.

SUPPORTS FOR CHILDREN WITH DYSGRAPHIA

In general, there are three ways that children with dysgraphia can be assisted to develop their fine motor skills:

* Carrying out exercises to improve fine motor movements of the hands.
* Using techniques to aid handwriting.
* Allowing the child to use other means of communication other than writing.

ROLE OF THE ELC PRACTITIONER

If you notice that a child in your setting is showing any of the symptoms of dysgraphia listed above, some of the following strategies may be useful:

* Engage the child in activities that help them 'feel' how letters are made. This can help children learn letter formation. For example, ask the child to close their eyes and trace the letter onto the palm of their hand. Practise this and then have the child try to trace the letter onto a page.
* Have the child 'write' letters in sand or add sand to finger paint and have them form letters on a page.
* Roll clay into ropes and practise making letters, or flatten out some clay and have the child etch letters into it.
* Children with dysgraphia often have difficulty with correct pencil grip. Spread some pieces of balled-up paper onto the table and have the child pick them up with tweezers.
* Children often find using a short pencil, e.g. a golf pencil or a pencil with a triangular grip, easier than a regular pencil.
* Activities that encourage coordinated movement can be beneficial before writing, e.g. arm windmills, jumping jacks, touching alternative toes or doing mountain climbers.
* Children with dysgraphia can have difficulty organising their thoughts. Practise reading stories to the child and having them retell the story in the correct sequence.
* As children get older, it helps if the child speaks what they want to say before they write. Use a smartphone or other device for recording.
* Children can begin to learn to use assistive technology, e.g. a laptop, in the setting.

3.8 EPILEPSY

Epilepsy is a neurological disorder that affects the brain. A person with epilepsy has seizures. There are different types of seizures depending on what part of the brain the seizure begins in, whether the person is aware that they are having a seizure and if there is movement while having the seizure.

PREVALENCE

Epilepsy is very common, with approximately 100,000 children in Ireland having epilepsy (Epilepsy Ireland, 2021).

CAUSES

While no cause can be determined for about half to three-quarters of the cases of epilepsy, common causes include genetic factors (some forms of epilepsy run in families), head injuries, infections of the brain and its coverings, e.g. meningitis, oxygen deprivation during prenatal, birth or postnatal stages. Epilepsy sometimes occurs with other additional needs, e.g. Down syndrome, autism, cerebral palsy and hydrocephalus.

SYMPTOMS

There are several different **types of seizure in children**. Paediatric seizures can be categorised as two broad types: focal and generalised.

Focal seizures, also called partial seizures, may be described as simple or complex. With focal seizures, particularly with complex focal seizures, the child may experience an aura before the seizure occurs. An aura is a strange feeling, either consisting of visual changes, hearing abnormalities or changes in the sense of smell. Simple focal seizures normally last less than a minute. Seizure activity is normally limited to an isolated motor group, e.g. legs, and consciousness is not lost. The child may also become pale, begin to sweat and feel nauseous. Complex focal seizures normally last one or two minutes. Consciousness is normally lost, and a variety of behaviours can occur in the child, e.g. gagging, lip smacking. The child will usually be sleepy after the seizure.

Generalised seizures involve both sides of the brain. There are six different types of generalised seizure:

* **Absence seizures:** the child will typically 'zone out' for a period of up to 30 seconds.

* **Atonic seizures:** there is a sudden loss of muscle tone and the child may suddenly fall or drop their head. This is why this type of seizure is commonly called a 'drop attack'.

* **Generalised tonic-clonic seizures:** the child will lose consciousness and the body, arms and legs will flex, extend and shake. The child will be very tired afterwards and may have a headache.

* **Myoclonic seizures:** this type of seizure refers to quick movements or sudden jerking of a group of muscles. These seizures tend to occur in clusters, meaning that they may occur several times a day, or for several days in a row.

* **Febrile seizures:** these seizures occur when children have a very high temperature. They are most commonly seen in children between six months and five years of age and there may be a family history of this type of seizure. Febrile seizures that last less than 15 minutes are called 'simple' and typically do not have long-term effects. Seizures lasting more than 15 minutes are called 'complex' and may cause long-term issues.

TREATMENT

Anti-epileptic drugs (AEDs) are the commonest treatment for epilepsy. These medications do not cure epilepsy, but rather they treat it and help stop the seizures from occurring. There are many different forms of AEDs. The type of AED prescribed will depend on the type of epilepsy the child has. When a child is first given an AED, it will be a very low dose. As time goes on, the dose will be gradually increased if required. This is to minimise the risk of side effects. While it is most desirable that patients be on only one drug to treat their epilepsy (monotherapy), some seizures prove difficult to control, so patients may have to take more than one AED (polytherapy).

ROLE OF THE ELC PRACTITIONER

If a child in an ELC setting has a seizure, it is very important that staff know what to do, particularly if the child has lost consciousness. It is, therefore, essential that staff receive adequate training. If a child has a seizure in the setting:

* Protect the child from injury (remove any harmful objects nearby).

* Cushion their head.

* Gently place the child in the recovery position.

* Time the length of the seizure.

* Stay with the child until recovery is complete.

* Calmly reassure the child.

An ambulance should be called if:

* It is the child's first seizure.

* The seizure continues for more than five minutes.

* One seizure follows another without the child gaining awareness.

* The child is injured or you believe the child needs medical attention.

Sometimes while a child is having a seizure, rescue drugs such as buccal midazolam are prescribed to stop the seizure. Staff should receive training in how to administer this drug. With buccal midazolam the contents of a pre-filled oral syringe are emptied into the space between the inside of the cheek and the lower gum. Staff caring for a child with epilepsy will be asked to keep a seizure diary recording information such as the date and time of seizure, type of seizure, duration of seizure and any possible triggers.

3.9 HYDROCEPHALUS

Hydrocephalus literally means 'water in the head' and is caused by an accumulation of cerebrospinal fluid (CSF) within the ventricles of the brain, resulting in raised pressure inside the head. At least 80% of those born with spina bifida have some degree of hydrocephalus and many premature babies also develop the condition. In babies and young children, the skull bones are not yet fused together, and the raised pressure causes the head to increase in size.

PREVALENCE

The overall prevalence of hydrocephalus is estimated to be 0.5% of all children, i.e. one in every 500 live births. There are two main types of hydrocephalus: congenital, i.e. present at birth, and acquired, i.e. occurring after birth.

CAUSES

There are believed to be over 180 causes of hydrocephalus, the commonest of which is premature birth. With a premature baby, the brain is still developing at birth, so the blood vessels of the brain are very fragile. Hydrocephalus is caused if the blood vessels become damaged, as this causes a build-up of fluid that cannot be drained effectively. Eighty per cent of children with spina bifida (see page 40), especially myelomeningocele (pronounced my-lo-men-in-jo-seal) and sometimes meningocele (pronounced men-in-jo-seal), have hydrocephalus. Meningitis is an infection of the linings or meninges of the brain and spinal cord and this infection can cause hydrocephalus. The debris and inflammation or swelling caused by the infection can cause blockages of the drainage pathways of the brain and thus cause cerebrospinal fluid to build up. Brain and spinal tumours may also compress the brain and spinal cord, narrowing the drainage pathways and causing a cerebrospinal fluid build-up.

SYMPTOMS OR CHARACTERISTICS

Excessive head growth is a symptom of hydrocephalus. All babies should have their heads regularly measured and recorded on a percentile chart. A baby head with hydrocephalus will normally be above the 97th percentile, meaning that the head will be bigger than 97% of babies in the same age bracket.

* A bulging, tense fontanelle.
* A restless baby with a high-pitched, shrill cry.
* Vomiting.
* Sleepiness.
* Bulging eyes and uneven pupil size.
* Downward deviation of the eyes (also called sunsetting), where the baby appears to be looking at their bottom eyelids.
* Seizures.
* Delayed closing of the anterior fontanelle in the skull. This normally closes by ten to 14 months.

If hydrocephalus is left untreated, as it can be in many developing nations, then coma and death will occur. If treated (usually with the insertion of a shunt), it can be brought under control. Even if treated, hydrocephalus can cause developmental issues.

TREATMENT AND SUPPORTS FOR CHILDREN WITH HYDROCEPHALUS

The main treatment for hydrocephalus is the surgical insertion of a shunt (a small plastic tube) into the brain. The shunt works by draining fluid off the brain, either into the stomach or into the heart. The shunt will not be visible from the outside; there will only be a slightly raised area on the head behind the ear. As the child grows, their shunt will be regularly replaced. Early insertion of a shunt is vital so that brain damage does not occur. Shunts cannot repair damage that has already been done to the brain; they can only prevent further damage.

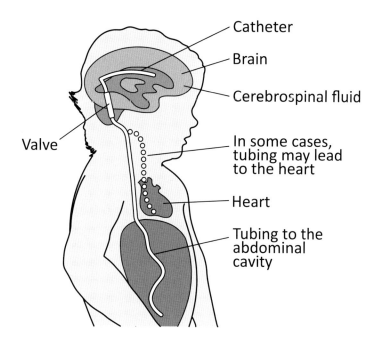

Catheter

Brain

Cerebrospinal fluid

Valve

In some cases, tubing may lead to the heart

Heart

Tubing to the abdominal cavity

ROLE OF THE ELC PRACTITIONER

Many children with hydrocephalus do not have any additional needs and therefore will not require any special assistance. However, ELC personnel need to be educated about the condition and be aware of the signs that the child's shunt is not functioning properly. Also, the setting personnel should ensure that the child does not get any knocks to the head, e.g. during rough-and-tumble play. For other children whose development is more affected by their hydrocephalus (particularly if there are other conditions present), there may be a wide range of needs that an ELC practitioner will have to assist with. These may include:

* Help with toileting.

* Mobility needs – the child may be in a wheelchair or have a frame.

* If the child has behavioural difficulties, more one-to-one attention may be required to help the child stay on task.

One of the most important roles of the ELC practitioner is to recognise the signs that there may be something wrong with the child's shunt. The following are the commonest signs that there is something wrong. (Please note, however, that each child is different, and that these are just the commonest symptoms.) Some symptoms will vary with the age of the child. If practitioners have any concerns, they should contact the child's parents/guardians immediately and seek medical assistance.

* Dividing of skull sutures (babies).
* Enlargement of the head (babies and toddlers).
* Fever (all).
* Full, tense fontanelle (babies).
* Headache (toddlers and children).
* Irritability (all).
* Lethargy and listlessness (children).
* Loss of bowel and bladder control (children).
* Personality change (children).
* Seizures (all).
* Sleepiness (toddlers and children).
* Staggering (children).
* Swelling or redness along the track of the shunt (all).
* Vomiting (toddlers and children).

3.10 MUSCULAR DYSTROPHY

Muscular dystrophy (MD) refers to a group of genetically inherited muscular diseases that weaken the muscles of the body. Muscular dystrophies are characterised by progressive weakening and wasting of the muscles of the body. There are at least nine different forms of muscular dystrophy of which Duchenne muscular dystrophy (DMD) first diagnosed by the French neurologist Guillaume Duchenne, is the commonest and unfortunately most severe form of the condition. Duchenne MD will be the focus of this section.

Extend your learning

Watch the YouTube clip 'Many faces of Duchenne muscular dystrophy' (3.35) to gain an understanding of the daily challenges that children with DMD face.

PREVALENCE

It is estimated that DMD affects approximately one in 3,500 male births. Girls can have the condition, but generally symptoms are much less severe.

Spina bifida myelomeningocele is the commonest form of spina bifida. The higher up on the spinal cord the split occurs the greater the problems the child will experience. With this form of spina bifida, the split is so large that the spinal cord and nerves bulge out into the balloon filled with fluid. The spinal cord and nerves become exposed and the degree of damage will determine the extent of disability. Myelomeningocele is most frequently found in the lumbar area but can occur anywhere along the spine.

Spina bifida myelomeningocele

Encephalocele (pronounced en-sef-a-lo-seal): in a small number of cases of neural tube defect, the split is high up and involves the back of the head (skull). There will be a balloon-like swelling, but this does not generally contain important nerves like the spinal column. Some encephaloceles are small and covered with skin and the children usually grow up without major implications. Sometimes, however, if it is large it may contain some brain tissue, which can severely affect the baby's eyesight and cause learning severe disabilities.

Anencephaly (pronounced an-en-sef-a-lee) is the severest neural tube defect. The skull does not form and the entire brain above the brainstem fails to develop. Unlike other forms of spina bifida, the condition is inoperable, and the prognosis is extremely poor. Due to the extent of brain damage, babies are unlikely to survive outside the uterus. They may be stillborn or die shortly after birth.

TREATMENT AND SUPPORTS FOR CHILDREN WITH SPINA BIFIDA MYELOMENINGOCELE

These may include:

* Surgery to repair the spinal column.
* Treatment of hydrocephalus with insertion of shunt.
* Physiotherapy to aid movement and prevent muscles from weakening further.
* Occupational therapy to help children master tasks required for everyday living.
* Mobility aids such as leg braces, walkers and wheelchairs.
* Surgery for bone and joint problems.
* Catheterisation to allow the child to urinate.
* Use of laxatives and suppositories to help with bowel movements.

ROLE OF ELC PRACTITIONER

The principal role of the ELC practitioner is catering for the child's physical care and mobility needs, and may include:

* Changing the baby's position to prevent pressure sores.

* Keeping the nappy area clean, dry and moisturised. Special attention must be paid to creases in the skin.

* Assisting older children with toileting, helping the child sit on the toilet safely, insertion of catheter, cleaning themselves properly and dressing themselves. Be aware of the child's need for privacy.

* Assisting the child to move around the setting.

3.13 VISION IMPAIRMENT

The World Health Organization (WHO) defines blindness as being unable to count fingers held up at 6 metres (20 feet) or less while the person is using the best correction possible.

PREVALENCE

Only about 10% of people who are termed legally blind have no vision at all. There are approximately 240 children under the age of 18 in Ireland today who are legally blind. In addition, there are approximately 4,700 children who, although not termed legally blind, have a vision impairment severe enough to be considered an additional need (National Council for the Blind in Ireland, 2021). In addition, 60–80% of children who are vision impaired have at least one other impairment or chronic illness (NCBI, 2021).

CAUSES

Vision impairment can be caused by failure of the eye to develop properly, damage to the eye itself or damage to the optic nerve or other parts of the nervous system connected to it, e.g. the visual cortex of the brain. These problems can arise at different times during a child's development.

BEFORE BIRTH:

* There may be a family history of blindness, whereby blindness is genetically inherited.

* Maternal rubella or other infections, such as syphilis, during pregnancy.

* Toxoplasmosis, an infection that comes from parasites found in animal faeces or undercooked meat. Therefore, pregnant women should avoid farm animals (or if they are in contact with them, should be extra cautious with personal hygiene) and lightly cooked meats. Some professionals also advise pregnant women to stay away from unpasteurised dairy products and shellfish that may swim in polluted waters.

AROUND BIRTH:

* Prematurity: babies born earlier than 35 weeks' gestation are at risk of eye defects.

* Infections, e.g. herpes simplex, during the birth process.

* Oxygen poisoning or toxicity (too much oxygen given at birth).

* Asphyxia during the birth process (deprived of oxygen at birth).

AFTER BIRTH:

* Head and eye injuries.

* Infections, e.g. measles.

* Cataracts (a clouding over the eye lens).

* Inflammatory diseases, e.g. conjunctivitis (untreated in developing world).

* Vitamin A deficiency (in the developing world).

STRUCTURE OF THE EYE

In order to understand the different types of vision impairment, a knowledge of the structure of the eye is important.

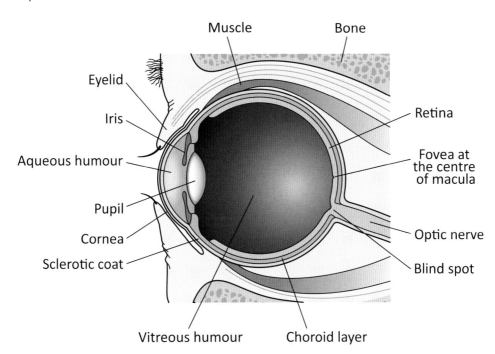

SYMPTOMS OR CHARACTERISTICS

Degrees of vision impairment will depend on what form the individual has. Listed below are the main types of vision impairment in the Western world. Patterns of vision impairment are different in developing nations, where more children are visually impaired as a result of environmental reasons (lack of vitamin A) or lack of medical care.

Albinism is a genetically inherited condition where the eyes, hair and skin lack normal levels of the pigment melanin. As the gene for albinism is usually recessive, both parents must be carriers of the gene, though some rare forms are inherited from only one parent. Also, there is a rare form of albinism called ocular albinism that affects only the eyes. It is carried on the X chromosome, so while females can be carriers, only males have the condition. Eye conditions common with albinism may include:

✳ Abnormal decussation (crossing) of the optic nerve fibres going to the brain.

✳ Amblyopia: This condition is sometimes incorrectly mixed up with strabismus and called lazy eye. This is not accurate, because with amblyopia, the eye is quite normal. It is the area of the brain meant to interpret visual images that is not working correctly.

✳ Astigmatism: the cornea of the eye is misshapen, resulting in blurred vision.

✳ Macular hypoplasia: underdevelopment of the fovea (area in the centre of the retina).

✳ Myopia (short-sightedness – difficulty seeing items far away) or hyperopia (long-sightedness – difficulty seeing close up).

✳ Nystagmus: irregular rapid movement of the eyes back and forth or in a circular motion.

✳ Optic nerve hypoplasia: underdevelopment of the optic nerve.

✳ Photophobia: hypersensitivity to bright light and glare.

✳ Strabismus: eye misalignment – crossed eyes or lazy eye. If left untreated (usually with special glasses or a patch), it can cause vision impairment and blindness.

Of course, all the above conditions can occur alone without albinism and cause visual impairment.

Extend your learning

In Tanzania, albinos represent one in every 1,429 births, a much higher rate than in any other nation. Tragically in Tanzania, rituals and spiritual ideas about albinism have led to attacks on and the brutal murder of innocent men, women and especially children. These ideas have been around for many generations, but in recent years witch doctors have been teaching misconceived ideas about the promise of wealth, success and power when albino hair or limbs are used in a potion as part of witchcraft practices. Go to YouTube and search 'Tanzanian children with albinism hunted for their body parts' to find videos on this horrendous practice.

Congenital blindness means blindness from birth. It can be inherited or caused by something that occurs during the prenatal period, e.g. the mother contracting rubella.

Congenital cataracts are present at birth and cause a clouding of the lens of the eye. Because the lens is cloudy, light cannot focus properly on the retina and sight is impaired. Cataracts at birth are rare and may be caused by maternal rubella or appear with other syndromes, e.g. Down syndrome. Cataracts will usually be removed shortly after birth unless they have been caused by maternal rubella, in which case they cannot be removed for several months. There is usually a lasting effect on vision, especially if caused by rubella.

Cortical visual impairment may cause total or partial blindness. Someone with cortical vision impairment alone will have nothing wrong with their eyes; rather, the brain does not process visual messages either properly or at all.

Glaucoma is a serious eye condition that results from the excessive build-up of pressure in the fluid of the eye. It is quite rare, occurring in approximately one in 10,000 children. As eye pressure builds up, the various parts of the eye, particularly the optic nerve, become damaged, thus resulting in blindness or partial blindness. Early symptoms of glaucoma include cloudy corneas, a prominent eye or eyes, sensitivity to bright light (tilting of the head away or eye closure), excessive tearing or one eye larger than the other. Glaucoma is usually treated with surgery and medication that reduces eye pressure. Unfortunately, damage caused before treatment is irreversible, so early detection is vital.

Retinitis pigmentosa is a genetically inherited progressive eye condition whereby the photoreceptors (rods and cones) located in the retina develop abnormally. The condition usually takes years to develop, although it can develop more quickly and therefore be a cause of vision impairment in children. Someone with retinitis pigmentosa will normally experience night blindness first (an inability to see in dim light), followed by a gradual reduction in perceptual vision (tunnel vision). Retinitis pigmentosa can cause total blindness if central vision becomes affected as well, although this rarely, if ever, occurs in children. There is no real effective treatment for the condition.

Retinopathy of prematurity (ROP) is an eye disorder that predominantly affects prematurely born babies. The blood vessels of the eye develop between the 16th and 36th week of pregnancy. Babies born prematurely can have a disorganised growth pattern of the blood vessels in the retina, which may result in scarring and retinal detachment (pulling the retina out of shape). Retinopathy of prematurity can be mild and may resolve spontaneously, but it may lead to blindness in serious cases. As such, all preterm babies are at risk of ROP. Very low birth weight babies (1 kg or 2.4 lb and under) are at additional risk. Both oxygen toxicity and oxygen deprivation can contribute to the development of ROP. All premature babies are examined for the condition, as early laser surgery can help prevent it worsening. If untreated, blindness or partial blindness can result. Even if treated, babies born with ROP are at a much greater risk of developing other eye conditions, e.g. glaucoma, cataracts, myopia and strabismus.

Extend your learning

For further information on eye conditions that cause visual impairment, see the Royal National Institute of Blind People website, www.rnib.org.uk. Click on Eye Health, then Eye Conditions, and you will find an A to Z list of conditions.

ROLE OF THE ELC PRACTITIONER

As with all children, the focus of the ELC practitioner should be on the active participation of the vision-impaired child in all activities. Because children with vision impairments may not be able to learn by watching what is going on around them, they must learn by 'doing' and physically interacting with their environment. The child should be given the opportunity to participate in all activities, and if they cannot participate independently the ELC practitioner must explore ways that the child can be assisted through the activity, being careful to observe and know what parts of the activity the child can do independently and allowing them to do so.

In order to learn about the world, a child with vision impairment needs experience with real objects, using the rest of their senses. Provide real objects where possible, especially when the child is learning a new concept, e.g. use real fruit and vegetables instead of plastic ones. When working with the child, talk about what is going on. Seat the child close to you at story time or circle time. For children with low vision, choose toys that have lights or bright colours with contrast. If using picture books, select one with colourful and simple pictures, rather than ones that are visually cluttered. If using photographs, use matt finish to reduce glare. Provide toys and learning materials that have a variety of textures, shapes, sizes and weights so that the child can make full use of their sense of touch. Provide toys that produce voice or noise, e.g. musical instruments or cause-and-effect toys. When walking around the setting, it is sometimes best if the child is barefoot so that they can get more information about their surroundings. It is important that different areas of the setting are well defined so that the child can easily orient themselves.

Children who are vision impaired and blind rely on their hands to learn about their world. It is therefore very important to provide plenty of activities that promote fine motor skills. Messy play allows children the opportunity to feel material with their hands, e.g. Play-Doh, mud, water or other materials. Sometimes it is good to allow the child to experience a new toy or activity on their own, giving them plenty of time to do so. Ensure that the room is well organised so that the child knows where various play items and materials are located. There are various learning resources, e.g. textured cups (see image below), that can be used to begin the process of learning braille. All registered vision-impaired children have access to a visiting teacher service. These teachers are experts in working with vision-impaired children and can advise practitioners in the setting about available resources.

Textured cups can be used to begin the process of learning braille.

SHOW YOU KNOW

Choose three of the following additional needs and write a note on each one under the headings prevalence, causes, symptoms, treatment and the role of the ELC practitioner:

* Asthma
* Cerebral palsy
* Cystic fibrosis
* Developmental dyspraxia
* Diabetes mellitus
* Dysgraphia

* Epilepsy
* Hydrocephalus
* Muscular dystrophy
* Sickle cell disease
* Spina Bifida
* Vision impairment

4

Additional Needs Affecting Intellectual Development

What I will learn

✻ Understand a range of additional needs that affect intellectual development.

4.1 INTRODUCTION

This chapter introduces additional needs that can impact on children's intellectual development. It explores how these additional needs can impact on a child's life and how effective ELC settings can support children's learning and development. The additional needs that will be addressed in this chapter are:

✻ General learning disability.

✻ Specific learning disability – dyscalculia.

4.2 GENERAL LEARNING DISABILITY (GLD)

A general learning disability can range from borderline mild, mild, moderate, to severe/profound. Children with general learning disabilities find it more difficult to learn, understand and do things than other children of the same age. They can continue to learn and to make progress all through their lives but at a slower pace than other children. A child with borderline mild or mild general learning disability has very different learning abilities and needs than a child with a moderate or a severe/profound learning disability (National Council for Special Education [NCSE], 2014).

PREVALENCE

Based on 2016 Census of Population figures, GLD has a prevalence rate of 5.96 per 1,000 population. The prevalence rate for mild intellectual disability (which traditionally has been under-reported) was 1.92 per 1,000, and the rate for moderate, severe or profound intellectual disability was 3.49 per 1,000.

CAUSES

There are many possible causes of learning disability including genetic factors, infection before birth, brain injury at birth, brain infection or damage after birth. More specific examples include Down syndrome, fragile X syndrome and cerebral palsy. In nearly half the children affected, the cause of the disability remains unknown, even after tests have been done.

SYMPTOMS OR CHARACTERISTICS

Children with a general learning disability will vary greatly in terms of the additional needs they present with.

Children with borderline and mild general learning disabilities mature and develop certain skills at a slower rate than other children. They may have difficulties with speech and language, developing concepts, and later have difficulty with reading, writing, numeracy and comprehension. They may find it difficult to adapt to ELC settings and later school life and may show signs of inappropriate or what might be considered immature behaviour for their age. They may experience difficulty making friends with other children their own age as they can lack the emotional and social skills required.

Children with a moderate GLD have impaired development and learning ability in respect of language and communication, social and personal development, motor coordination and basic literacy and numeracy as well as independent living skills. They may also have additional or multiple disabilities, such as physical impairment, hearing impairment, visual impairment, cerebral palsy, autism, emotional disturbance, sensory losses or behavioural problems.

Children with severe and profound general learning disabilities show very significant delays in reaching developmental milestones. Their basic awareness and understanding of themselves and the world around them is limited by their level of disability. Children with this level of disability may depend on others throughout their lives to help them with basic needs, such as mobility, communication, feeding and toileting.

SUPPORTING CHILDREN WITH GENERAL LEARNING DISABILITY

Parents of any child born after 1 June 2002 may apply to the HSE for an Assessment of Need under the Disability Act if they think that their child may have a disability. Following the assessment, parents receive an Assessment Report stating their child's needs and the services required to meet those needs. The types of services and supports put in place for children with a general learning disability will depend on whether the disability is borderline, mild, moderate, severe or profound.

Since 2010, the Irish State has funded a free pre-school place for all eligible children in the year prior to starting school through the Early Childhood Care and Education (ECCE) Programme. Since 2016, the access and inclusion model (AIM) of pre-school education and care has meant that children with disabilities now have access to and are supported to participate meaningfully in the ECCE programme in pre-school settings nationwide. The goal of AIM is to empower providers to create a more inclusive environment for all children, regardless of ability. Under this model the following supports are available:

* Specialist advice and supports.

* Specialist equipment and appliances.

* Funding for minor building alterations.

* Therapeutic interventions and in a small number of cases extra assistance in the ELC setting.

* Continuous professional development programmes for staff, e.g. The Leadership for Inclusion in Early Years Care (LINC) qualification led by Mary Immaculate College in Limerick.

When children reach school-going age, where they will access education will depend on the level of their general learning disability. Children with borderline mild and mild general learning disability normally access mainstream education where they also access additional learning support. Some children may also attend a special class attached to a mainstream school. Some, particularly those with moderate, severe or profound general learning disability, attend special schools where staff have specialist knowledge and experience of working with children with general learning disabilities.

THE ROLE OF THE ELC PRACTITIONER

The role of the ELC practitioner will again depend on the child's level of general learning disability. The following general strategies will apply for children with borderline, mild and moderate general learning disabilities:

* Establish a supportive and trusting relationship with the child.

* Focus on what the child can do rather than what they cannot do and build on these strengths.

* Give plenty of praise and encouragement.

* Simplify language, repeat words and clarify meanings.

* Observe the child closely and offer activities that they will be able to do so that they experiences success.

* Present activities and tasks in small sequential steps – show rather than tell.

* Find out what interests and excites the child and use this information as the basis of activities and tasks.

* Introduce one new skill at a time and allow plenty of opportunity for repetition and overlearning. (Overlearning is rehearsing a skill over and over until it is very well known.)

* Give opportunity for the learning of life skills, e.g. dressing, washing hands, feeding, etc.

The following general strategies may be useful for children with severe or profound general learning disabilities:

* The child should have a very specific individual learning and care plan.

* A responsive environment should be created in which the child's actions are always acknowledged, e.g. if the child smiles then the ELC practitioner should acknowledge this, saying, for example: 'Aaron is very happy today.'

* Objects of reference can be used to represent activities, places and people, e.g. a spoon could be used to signal snack time, or a picture of the garden could be used to signal 'We are going outside'.

* Alternative communication systems may be used, e.g. Lámh signing system, the Picture Exchange Communication System (PECS) and electronic communication devices.

* The setting should have provision for taking medication and/or special diet.

* Setting layout should allow for use of specialist equipment, e.g. wheelchairs.

* Communication between home and school is vital to ensure that what is being offered in the setting is meeting the child's needs.

* Children with severe and profound general disabilities may have significant care needs, e.g. toileting, feeding, etc.

PECS board

4.3 SPECIFIC LEARNING DISABILITY – DYSCALCULIA

Dyscalculia is a specific learning disability whereby the child (and later adult) has an innate difficulty in learning or comprehending mathematics. In some ways, it is to mathematics what dyslexia is to reading, writing and spelling.

PREVALENCE

Current estimates suggest that dyscalculia may affect about 5% of the population. However, some psychologists suspect that at least some children diagnosed with dyscalculia may not have the disability at all, and instead their difficulties with mathematics are due to environmental factors resulting in an intense dislike and/or fear of mathematics, avoiding the subject if possible. As a result, the child gets little practice and falls further behind, continuing the cycle of dislike and avoidance.

CAUSES

It is not known what causes dyscalculia. It tends to run in families, indicating a genetic component but researchers continue to try to work out the differences between children whose problems with maths stem from deficits in brain processing (dyscalculia) and those whose problems are related to factors such as poor instruction, poverty or coexisting conditions. Research has also found that, for people with maths anxiety, the anticipation of having to do a maths activity triggers the same centres in the brain that register threat and physical pain. Since this was not observed during the actual performance of maths problems, researchers suspect the mere anticipation of maths is more anxiety-provoking than the maths itself and can cause those affected to try to avoid maths problems altogether (Lyons *et al.*, 2012).

SYMPTOMS OR CHARACTERISTICS

As with dyslexia, a child under six will not yet have been assessed for dyscalculia. However, some of the following indicators may be present in children aged 3–5 years.

* Difficulty recognising numbers.
* Delayed learning to count.
* Struggle to connect numerical symbols to words, e.g. five and 5.
* May have difficulty recognising patterns.
* May have difficulty placing things in order, e.g. smallest to largest.
* May lose track when counting.
* Difficulty classifying, i.e. grouping similar items together.
* Difficulty matching similar items and sets of items, e.g. if a child is shown a place setting (knife, fork, dessert spoon and cup), they may have difficulty copying it.
* Difficulty understanding position, e.g. over, under, up, down, on, in, beside and between.
* Difficulty with concepts connected to time, i.e. morning/evening, night/day, days of the week, etc.

SYMPTOMS OR CHARACTERISTICS

In babies, the symptoms of hearing loss will normally be that they do not reach their expected milestones for language and social development. Below are listed the expected milestones from birth to two years. A profoundly deaf baby will not reach these milestones. Babies with mild or moderate hearing loss may reach many of these milestones, which is why their hearing loss sometimes goes undetected, but will generally have less distinctive speech.

Did you know?

Since 2013, all babies born in Ireland are now screened for hearing loss. The type of test administered is called the Automated Otoacoustic Emissions (AOAE) test. The test is normally carried out before the baby leaves hospital. Another test, called the Automated Auditory Brainstem Response (AABR) test, may be administered in addition if a baby has an incomplete response to the AOAE test.

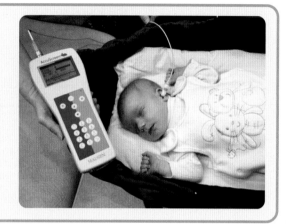

EXPECTED HEARING MILESTONES FROM BIRTH TO TWO YEARS

* **Zero to four months:** stops movement or quiets in response to speech or unfamiliar noises. Startles at loud sounds. Moves eyes towards sound source. Is roused from light sleep by sudden loud noises. Imitates gurgling or cooing sounds and shows a response to noise-making toys. At three months, the child should soothe or show responses to the carer's voice.

* **Four to seven months:** begins turning head towards sounds and voices out of sight (four months) and turns head directly towards the sound source (seven months). Smiles in response to speech. Looks in response to own name. Babbling begins.

* **Seven to nine months:** turns to find a sound source out of sight. Gurgles or coos to sounds out of sight. Tuneful babbling. Understands 'no'. Babbles in multiple syllables. Responds to own name. Responds to household sounds such as the bath filling – may get excited. At nine months, the child should engage in loud shrieking and sustained production of vowels.

* **Nine to 12 months:** acquires first true word, usually Dada. Imitates sounds. Looks at a familiar object when named, e.g. 'Where's Daddy?' Responds to music. Understands simple commands or requests, e.g. 'Give Mammy the spoon.' Uses own voice to get attention.

* **13 to 18 months:** uses sentence-like intonation – voice goes up and down as if they are speaking real sentences. Perceives emotions of others. Uses three to 20 words. Uses all vowels and consonants in jargon.

* **19 to 24 months:** uses more words than jargon. Asks questions by rising intonation at end of phrase. Comprehends about 300 words and uses about 50 words. Produces animal sounds. May combine two words into phrases, e.g. 'Doggy bold.' Listens to simple stories.

In older children, the symptoms of hearing impairment or loss are as follows:

* People have to raise their voice consistently to get the child's attention.

* The child frequently says 'huh?' or 'what?' when somebody is speaking.

* The child has a history of ear infections, often getting earaches or runny ears. The child complains of their ears hurting and about certain pitches of sound.

* The child watches the speaker's face carefully. The child turns their head so that one ear is facing the direction of the sound source.

* The child speaks very loudly.

* The child turns the TV up very loudly and sits very close to it.

* The child does not consistently look when called.

* The child confuses sounds that are alike, e.g. if a parent asks 'What about the bread?' the child responds, 'I made my bed.'

* The child's speech is unclear and poorer than would be expected for their age.

* The child is very quiet, using little verbal language.

* The child seems inattentive, frequently daydreaming.

* The child may become disruptive at pre-school or school, especially at times when children are involved in listening activities, e.g. story time.

SUPPORTS FOR CHILDREN WITH A HEARING IMPAIRMENT

Treatment depends on the type and degree of hearing loss.

HEARING AIDS

Once a child's hearing has been assessed it will be determined if hearing aids will help. Hearing aids amplify all sounds; however, hearing aids will be programmed to focus on maximising access to speech sounds. Usually two hearing aids are worn. There are several types of hearing aid.

* **Behind-the-ear hearing aids** (BTE), as the name suggests, are worn behind the ear and are connected to a custom-made silicone or acrylic ear mould that fits inside the outer ear. The components are held in a case behind the ear. Most children are fitted with digital BTE hearing aids due to technical advantages over in-the-ear hearing aids. Sound is picked up by the microphones, is amplified within the digital processing system and travels through the ear mould into the ear. BTE aids are used by people of all ages with mild to profound hearing loss.

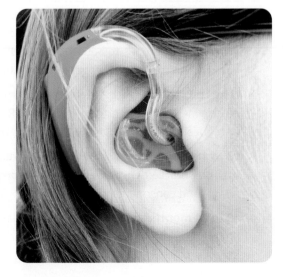

* **Behind-the-ear open fitting hearing aids** are used if a child's hearing loss is in the mild to moderate range. This still includes a BTE aid. Instead of using an ear mould, a very thin tube passes the sound into the ear canal, and this is held in position by a small dome.

* **A bone-anchored hearing aid:** conventional hearing aids are not suitable for some children, e.g. those with no ear canals (atresia). A bone-anchored hearing aid (BAHA) is used by some children and adults who cannot wear a conventional hearing aid. A BAHA can be worn on a headband behind the ear or can be surgically attached to the skull bone behind the ear. The BAHA works by transmitting sound through the skull bones directly to the cochlea. Children will normally have a trial with a test BAHA device on a headband (called a soft band), which allows parents and the audiologist to see how the child is responding. For young children, the soft band may be the best option until the child is old enough to undergo surgery for the device. A BAHA consists of three parts:

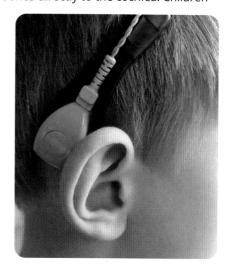

  * An implant, which is a small titanium screw implanted into the skull behind the ear.

  * An abutment, which is a socket attached to the implant.

  * A sound processor, which snaps onto the abutment.

* **Cochlear implant:** if a child's hearing loss is severe or profound, then high-powered digital hearing aids may not provide enough access to sounds for a child to be able to develop spoken language, and a cochlear implant may be an option. The principle behind the implant is that if someone's cochlear is so damaged that it cannot be stimulated and in turn stimulate the auditory nerve naturally by sound, the auditory nerve must be stimulated directly. Implants are composed of four parts; three are outside the body (external) and one is under the skin near the auditory nerve (internal):

  * A microphone, which picks up sound from the environment (external).

  * A speech processor, which is a little box normally held in a small backpack or pouch. The processor selects and arranges sounds picked up by the microphone.

  * A transmitter and receiver/stimulator, which receives signals from the speech processor and converts them into electric impulses (external).

  * An electrode array (surgically placed under the skin in the cochlea), which collects the impulses from the stimulator and sends them to different regions of the auditory nerve.

When the child has recovered from surgery, the implant will be turned on and the child begins the process of learning how to understand and use the new sounds they are hearing. It is best that the child receives the implant as early as possible in their lives, when the brain is most receptive to sound and language learning, although implants have been carried out on all age groups.

Did you know?

Ireland's first cochlear implant was completed in 1995, by the implant team in Beaumount Hospital, Dublin. Since then, over 1,000 implants have been completed there on all age groups from a few months to over 80 years of age (Beaumount Hospital website, 2021).

IRISH SIGN LANGUAGE (ISL)

Irish Sign Language is the first and preferred language of deaf people in Ireland. Just as other languages exist – French, German, etc. – so do other sign languages, e.g. British and American sign language. Cued Speech, Lámh and Signed English are not forms of ISL but are language-support systems based on English. ISL is a more natural language for a deaf person as it uses the entire body, hands and facial expressions.

Extend your learning

The Irish Deaf Society provides QQI-certified classes in Irish sign language. Go to their website to find out more: www.irishdeafsociety.ie.

THE ROLE OF THE ELC PRACTITIONER

It is important to understand that every child with a hearing impairment is different, with varying levels of hearing loss, different hearing aids, implants and communication preferences. It is therefore vital that practitioners consult with the child's parents/guardians extensively before the child enrols. In general, however, the following strategies should be borne in mind.

* To get the child's attention, wave or tap lightly on their shoulder.

* Get down to the child's level so that they can see your face clearly. Do not move around while you are speaking to the child as this will make it more difficult for them to hear your voice and to lip-read.

* Speak clearly and naturally. Speaking slowly or loudly makes lip-reading more difficult.

* Do not cover your mouth with your hands. Eating or chewing gum can also make lip-reading difficult.

* Use visual cues when possible, e.g. if you are telling the children it is time for lunch, using a knife and fork action could help.

* Ensure that the child knows what the topic of conversation is and make sure the child knows when the topic changes.

* Stand with your face to the light. Shadow or poor lighting makes lip-reading difficult.

* Group conversations can be difficult for the child to follow. Ask everyone to take turns to speak.

* Reduce background noise, e.g. do not have a radio on in the background. Shut out street noise by closing windows.

Extend your learning

Radio aids can be very useful, particularly when the child goes to school and there are many children in the classroom. The practitioner or teacher wears a microphone and a transmitter that is connected to the child's hearing aid. The teacher's voice is then transmitted to the child's hearing aid without all the background noise.

Soundfield systems can also be used. With this system, the practitioner or teacher's voice is amplified through speakers to the whole class. This helps all children, e.g. children who have temporary low hearing due to an ear infection.

5.3 SPECIFIC SPEECH AND LANGUAGE IMPAIRMENT

Note: The Irish Department of Education and Skills refers to this as specific speech and language disorder.

Specific speech and language impairment (SLI) is a developmental language impairment that can affect either expressive (spoken), receptive (understanding) language or both (called a global impairment). SLI is defined as a pure language impairment, meaning that it is not related to or caused by other developmental issues, e.g. cognitive impairment, hearing loss or acquired brain injury.

PREVALENCE

There are considerable variations reported in literature as to the prevalence of specific speech and language impairment. Most sources report a prevalence of 5% (Law *et al.*, 2000).

CAUSES

The cause of specific language impairment is not known. It tends to run in families (although not always), so there seems to be a strong genetic link.

SYMPTOMS OR CHARACTERISTICS

There are three different types of specific speech and language impairment, each of which has a different presentation:

* Expressive speech and language impairment.
* Receptive speech and language impairment.
* Global speech and language impairment.

Expressive speech and language impairment is characterised by limited vocabulary and a poor grasp of grammar. The child's understanding of language is likely to be far superior to their ability to communicate using the spoken word. They will be reluctant to talk and may resort to pointing or gesturing to get their message across. What the child does say often lacks variation in intonation or volume – it may sound flat. Imaginative play and social use of language may be further impaired. The child often only speaks when asked a specific, direct question, replying in very short, basic sentences. They will have difficulties in describing, defining and explaining and in retelling stories/events. Limited vocabulary may result in the child using empty repetitive phrases and non-specific words.

Receptive speech and language impairment is characterised by problems understanding oral language or in listening. Children will have difficulty processing and retaining information they hear and in following instructions and directions. Difficulties in understanding what is said will be worse in group situations or where there is a lot of background noise, which is a normal feature of ELC settings. Children will have difficulty answering questions because of difficulty processing the language of the question. Poor sound discrimination may also be evidenced, whereby the child will not hear the differences between similar-sounding words.

Global speech and language impairment is characterised by difficulties with both expressive and receptive language.

SUPPORTS FOR CHILDREN WITH SPECIFIC SPEECH AND LANGUAGE IMPAIRMENT

Treatment usually focuses on directly teaching the child the specific skills with which they are having difficulty. This work will be led by a speech and language therapist and will be supported by parents and the ELC setting the child is attending. Normally, children learn language almost automatically without any direct teaching. Children with SLI will have to be taught language more directly.

Extend your learning

Aspects of language
- **Phonology:** sounds of language.
- **Morphology:** grammar of the language, e.g. cat means one, cats means more than one.
- **Syntax:** word order in sentences, e.g. John hit the cat, the cat hit John – word order changes meaning.
- **Semantics:** the meaning of words and sentences.
- **Pragmatics:** knowing how to use language appropriately, e.g. turn taking, tone and volume of voice in different situations, eye contact, knowing when it is appropriate to change topic.

ROLE OF THE ELC PRACTITIONER

It is important to understand that every child with a specific speech and language impairment is different. Some may have more difficulty with expressive language and others with receptive language. It is therefore vital that practitioners consult with the child's parents/guardians extensively before the child enrols. In general, though, the following strategies should be borne in mind.

For a child who has predominantly a receptive language impairment:

* Use picture clues where appropriate.

* Use picture calendars to help the child to remember the daily routine.

* Sit the child close to you during activities that are language-dependent e.g. story time.

* Choose stories that have descriptive pictures and let the the child see these clearly. This will help the child to understand better what is being said.

* Before initiating a conversation with the child, it is important to make eye contact.

* Use simple sentence structures and a slower rate of speech.

* Use repetition, gesture and rephrasing of sentences to aid the child's understanding.

For a child who has predominantly an expressive language impairment:

* Give the child plenty of time to speak.

* Encourage the retelling of stories and events.

* Sometimes the use of puppets can help children gain confidence, e.g. the child may enjoy giving the puppet instructions or telling them about events.

* Books with pictures and photographs of familiar objects and activities from home can give the child confidence and remind them of things they can talk about.

* Expand what the child is saying, e.g. if the child says 'woman drive', the ELC practitioner may expand this to 'Yes. The woman is driving a new car.'

* Use of forced alternatives, e.g. at snack time, ask 'Do you want orange juice or milk?'

* Use of sentence closure, e.g. the ELC practitioner requires the child to finish the sentence 'I am drinking tea, you are drinking ...'

Extend your learning

Nationwide there are over 50 special classes attached to mainstream primary schools to support children who have a specific speech and language impairment. Go to the NCSE website and find out where the closest class is to where you live: https://ncse.ie/.

5.4 DYSLEXIA

There are many definitions of dyslexia. A very simple one would be that dyslexia is a specific learning difficulty that makes it more difficult for the individual to learn to read, write and spell well and that these difficulties are unexplained in relation to their other abilities and educational experiences.

A sample of dyslexic writing. This is the translation: Ellen must drink her milk. Stephen had a picnic of ham sandwiches. What are you two doing here? The flowers have many buds on them. Some people come here every day.

PREVALENCE

There is debate among professionals as to how prevalent dyslexia is. Approximately 20% of children in Irish schools have literacy difficulties (10% are judged to have serious difficulties). This figure rises to 50% in areas of poverty and social disadvantage (with 25 to 30% of children in these areas having serious reading difficulties). How many of these children have dyslexia and how many of them have literacy difficulties owing to other reasons is up for debate. Estimates for the prevalence of dyslexia (both mild and more severe) vary widely at between 4 and 10%.

CAUSES

Dyslexia tends to run in families. It appears to be linked to certain genes that affect how the brain processes reading and language, as well as risk factors in the environment. Dyslexia risk factors include:

* A family history of dyslexia or other learning disabilities.

* Premature birth or low birth weight.

* Exposure during pregnancy to nicotine, drugs, alcohol or infection that may alter brain development in the foetus.

* Individual differences in the parts of the brain that enable reading.

SYMPTOMS OR CHARACTERISTICS

Children in an ELC setting will obviously not yet have a diagnosis of dyslexia. However, the presence of several characteristics in children aged 3–5 may indicate that a child is at risk and should be closely monitored and allowed to learn at their own pace. It is vital that a child is not given a negative early experience of preliteracy. When considering these characteristics, however, be mindful that no child will have all these characteristics, that some are more common than others, and that all children will have some of these characteristics and not be exhibiting signs of dyslexia at all.

SPEAKING AND LISTENING

* Is later than most children learning to speak.
* Has difficulty pronouncing some words, especially monosyllabic words.
* Has difficulty separating spoken words into sounds and blending sounds to make words.
* Confuses some language sounds, e.g. fan and van.
* Is prone to spoonerisms e.g. chish and fips for fish and chips.
* Has difficulty with rhyming.
* Is unable to recall the correct word for something known to them.
* Is slow to add new vocabulary.
* May have difficulty telling or retelling a story in the correct sequence.

EARLY LITERACY

* Exhibits delays in acquiring emergent literacy skills, e.g. understanding that written language progresses from left to right and discriminating between letters.
* Experiences problems learning the alphabet.
* Has difficulty learning to write and spell their own name.

MEMORY

* Has difficulty learning numbers, days of the week, colours and shapes.
* Has difficulty following multistep directions or routines.

MOTOR COORDINATION

* Has difficulty maintaining rhythm.
* Delayed in developing fine motor skills.

(NCSE, 2021)

Extend your learning

The Special Education Support Service (SESS) and NCSE have created an informative introductory video on dyslexia . Go online and search 'Understanding Dyslexia – A Guide for Schools' (34.13) to see this video.

SUPPORTS FOR CHILDREN WITH DYSLEXIA

As children under six will not yet have a diagnosis of dyslexia, supports are generally not availed of until after the child starts school. If a diagnosis of dyslexia has been made, the child is likely to need extra tuition. The options available fall into two categories: school-based supports and supports outside school.

SCHOOL-BASED SUPPORTS

Support from the class teacher: The class teacher has an important role to play in being aware and considerate of each student's strengths and weaknesses. There are many things the class teacher can do to help teach a child with dyslexia more effectively.

Learning support teacher: Students with dyslexia that is not severe enough to qualify for resource teaching or a special reading school/unit may receive additional support in their school from the learning support teacher. This help is usually in a small group setting and is organised on a withdrawal basis from the regular class. Generally, students whose reading and spelling fall below the 12th percentile but above the second percentile are entitled to help from the learning support teacher.

Enrolment in a special reading school: Special reading schools are full-time Department of Education and Skills-funded primary schools. However, there are only four of them nationwide. The regular school curriculum is followed, except for Irish. The current pupil-to-teacher ratio is 9:1 and children usually attend for one to two years, depending on their progress, and then return to their own school. The usual criterion for admission to a special reading school is average/above average intelligence and a significant discrepancy between intellectual ability and literacy levels. The pupil should have completed second class or be at least eight years old and not more than 12 years old.

Enrolment in a special reading class attached to a mainstream primary school: There are a total of 23 special reading classes attached to mainstream primary schools in Ireland (as of July 2021). The ratio in these classes is 11:1. As with the four reading schools, children attend the reading class for one to two years, depending on need. Following a period of intense intervention children then return to their own primary school or to the mainstream part of the primary school to which the reading class is attached. Visit the NCSE website for a full list of these classes.

SUPPORTS OUTSIDE OF SCHOOL

The Dyslexia Association of Ireland (DAI) provides out-of-school support for children with dyslexia. This support takes two forms:

* Support on a one-to-one basis from a DAI-trained tutor.
* Enrolment in a DAI workshop, exam class and summer schools.

THE ROLE OF THE ELC PRACTITIONER

During the early years, because children have not begun formally to read and write, a diagnosis of dyslexia will be very unlikely. If a child in an ELC setting is, however, showing some of the characteristics listed in the 'symptoms' section, the following strategies may be used.

Develop listening skills by actively listening to the sounds around and identifying them – the telephone, pots and pans, water, doorbell, clapping, footsteps, animal and bird sounds. Tell or read stories, fairy tales and nursery rhymes every day in the setting. Help children develop an ear for rhymes by singing rhyming songs and reciting short rhymes with them.

Learn to listen to the sounds in words by talking about rhyming words and how they sound alike. Say pairs of words and ask if they rhyme, or use paired picture cards, e.g. ask 'Do cat and rat rhyme?' Encourage children to find words that rhyme, e.g. ask 'What words rhyme with bee?' Talk about words that start with the same sound. Say pairs of words and ask the child if they begin with the same sound, e.g. ask 'Do cat and car begin with the same sound? Do car and truck begin with the same sound?' Encourage children to find words that begin with the same sound, e.g. ask 'What words begin with the same sound as bag?' Play oral word games, e.g. 'I spy something that begins like bag'; 'What's the odd one out: pencil, pen, crayon?'

Develop speaking skills by taking time each day to talk with the child. Look at pictures and encourage the child to describe what they see. Encourage the retelling of stories and events.

Develop pre-reading skills by reading stories together each day. Help the child identify parts of the book, i.e. the top and bottom of the page, that the writing goes from left to right, important features such as capital letters, full stops and question marks. Display words all around the ELC environment, e.g. water area, sand area, etc. Help children to begin to recognise letters by using Play-Doh, magnetic letters, painting or drawing letters, tracing in wet sand. Provide plenty of opportunities for pre-writing activities and have the children 'read' what they have written.

Letter recognition can be supported by using sandpaper letters or tracing letters in wet sand. Practise word recognition skills, e.g. make word cards with the word printed on the front and a picture clue on the back. These cards can be used to play word recognition games.

SHOW YOU KNOW

Choose one of the following additional needs and write a note on it under the headings prevalence, causes, symptoms, treatment and the role of the ELC practitioner:

* Hearing impairment
* Specific speech and language impairment
* Dyslexia

Additional Needs Affecting Social and Emotional Development

What I will learn

* Understand a range of additional needs that affect social and emotional development.

6.1 INTRODUCTION

This chapter introduces additional needs that can impact on children's emotional and social development. It explores how these additional needs can impact on a child's life and how effective ELC settings can support children's learning and development in these settings. The additional needs that will be addressed in this chapter are:

* Attention Deficit and Hyperactivity Disorder (ADHD)
* Oppositional Defiant Disorder (ODD)

6.2 ATTENTION DEFICIT AND HYPERACTIVITY DISORDER (ADHD)

Attention deficit hyperactivity disorder (ADHD) is one of the commonest childhood disorders and can continue through adolescence and adulthood. Symptoms include difficulty staying focused and paying attention, difficulty controlling behaviour and hyperactivity (overactivity). Parents, teachers and others who work and live with children know that all children:

* Sometimes have difficulty controlling their behaviour.
* Sometimes have difficulty paying attention.
* Can be hyperactive and noisy from time to time.
* Can be impulsive.

However, the difference is that children with ADHD have these problems all the time. Behaviours are so intense that they interfere with the child's ability to function in many environments, in e.g. the ELC setting or the classroom, and with the child's ability to get along with other children.

PREVALENCE

It is estimated that 5% of children have ADHD (Fanning, 2020) with three to four times more boys having it than girls.

CAUSES

While the precise cause of ADHD is not clear, it is now known that it is a predominantly genetically inherited condition (a child with ADHD has a one in four chance of having a parent who also has ADHD). In terms of biological causes, magnetic resonance imaging (MRI) scans of the brain show differences between the brains of people with ADHD and the rest of the population. In people with ADHD, the right side of the brain is often smaller. Another type of brain scan, positron emission tomography (PET), has been used to obtain pictures of brain activity during tasks requiring concentration. Again, these show differences between those with ADHD and others. ADHD can also be influenced by environmental factors such as alcohol, drug use or smoking during pregnancy, which causes toxins to build up, thus harming the baby's brain. While factors such as poor parenting, a disruptive home life, too much TV or computer games and disruptive school environments cannot cause ADHD, they may cause the symptoms to worsen.

SYMPTOMS OR CHARACTERISTICS

The three major symptoms of ADHD are inattention, hyperactivity and impulsivity.

CHILDREN WHO ARE INATTENTIVE:

* Find it hard to keep their mind on what they are doing.
* Get bored or distracted with a task after a very short period of time.
* Find it hard to get started on tasks that require mental effort.
* Make careless mistakes and don't seem to care about details.
* Don't seem to listen when you talk to them.
* Don't follow through when given instructions.
* Don't get things finished.
* Are disorganised.
* Frequently lose or misplace things.
* However, they may be able to give effortless, automatic attention to something they enjoy, such as computer games or art activities.

CHILDREN WHO ARE HYPERACTIVE:

* Are moving all the time.

* Can't sit still.

* Squirm in their seat, swing their legs, tap their fingers or pencil on the table.

* Talk too much and often very quickly, jumping from one topic to the next.

* Run, jump and climb, even when this is not allowed, e.g. in a church or at school.

* Cannot play quietly.

CHILDREN WHO ARE IMPULSIVE:

* Do things without thinking, e.g. they may run out into the street without checking for traffic.

* Blurt out inappropriate comments.

* Shout out answers.

* Interrupt other people.

* Find it hard to wait their turn.

As a result of these behaviours, children with ADHD can often develop social and emotional problems and may experience low self-esteem or feel angry. Many find it difficult to make friends because of their frequent disruptive and socially inappropriate behaviour.

ADHD has three subtypes:

1. Predominantly hyperactive-impulsive.

2. Predominantly inattentive. Children in this category are often described as having attention deficit disorder (ADD). In the main they will not be hyperactive; in fact, the opposite can be the case.

3. Combined hyperactive-impulsive and inattentive. This subtype is the commonest. These children will have many of the symptoms described in all three categories.

In addition to ADHD, many children have other conditions as well. Conditions that commonly occur with ADHD are:

* Dyslexia (see chapter 5)

* Dyscalculia (see chapter 4)

* Dysgraphia (see chapter 3)

* Dyspraxia (see chapter 3)

* Difficulty with auditory perception

* Specific language difficulties (see chapter 5)

* Oppositional defiant disorder (see below)

* Anxiety, depression and obsessive-compulsive disorder

* Occasionally, children with Asperger's or Tourette syndrome are incorrectly diagnosed with ADHD.

SUPPORTING CHILDREN WITH ADHD

ADHD is normally treated using a combination of stimulant medication and behavioural therapy.

Medication: Several stimulant medications are available which calm the child, allowing them to bring their behaviour under better control. Many people are surprised to learn that stimulants are given to children with ADHD, as these children seem to be overstimulated already, but such treatment is effective. Ritalin, perhaps the best-known ADHD medication, has been widely used since its release in 1954. Other trade names include Adderall, Dexedrine and Metadate.

Stimulants work by increasing dopamine levels in the brain, and one of the functions of dopamine is to control attention. It also controls motivation, pleasure and movement. By regulating the dopamine levels, doctors can regulate the attention spans and energy levels of those they are treating. A smaller number of children are prescribed non-stimulant medications, e.g. Strattera.

Talk therapies: Counselling can prove very beneficial for children and young adults with ADHD as they can begin to understand their condition and talk about their feelings and the ways in which the issues that they are experiencing can be managed more effectively.

Behavioural therapies: Behavioural therapy can be used alone or with medication, as described above. Basically, behavioural therapy is designed to teach children to control their hyperactivity, impulsiveness and lack of attention. Based on the work of B. F. Skinner, desirable behaviour is rewarded (positively reinforced) and undesirable behaviour is not reinforced to discourage its repetition.

ROLE OF THE ELC PRACTITIONER

Children with ADHD can have difficulty staying focused and paying attention, controlling behaviour and being hyperactive (overactive). The following strategies may be used by ELC practitioners to help the child control their behaviour and stay more focused:

* Research and gain a good understanding of ADHD. Build up a good relationship with parents/guardians and work in partnership with them.

* Always show patience and tolerance. Speak in a calm voice.

* Routine, consistency and predictability is very important for all young children, but particularly those with ADHD.

* Children (especially those with ADHD) work best in an organised, well-structured physical environment where materials and equipment are neatly and predictably stored.

* Find out what the child's interests are and build tasks and activities around these interests.

* Set clear rules and boundaries. There should not be too many of them and they should be phrased in a positive way, e.g. 'Put away one toy before using another one.'

* Present tasks and activities in a step-by-step fashion and praise the child for completion of each step.

* Sometimes an egg timer is useful to help the child's concentration skills.

* Catch the child being good as often as possible and reinforce positive work and behaviour. A rewards chart can be useful.

* Use positive language when interacting with the child. Explain to the child what it is you want them to do rather than what you want them not to do or to stop doing.

* Ignore minor behaviours and avoid over-reporting poor behaviours to parents/guardians.

* Recognise when the child with ADHD is becoming overstimulated and provide movement breaks, e.g. in the garden area.

* Provide as much one-to-one attention as possible.

* When involved in group activities it may be best to sit the child close to you.

6.3 OPPOSITIONAL DEFIANT DISORDER (ODD)

Oppositional defiant disorder (ODD) is characterised by an ongoing pattern of disobedient, hostile and defiant behaviour toward authority figures that goes beyond the bounds of normal childhood behaviour. For a child to be diagnosed with ODD, certain factors must be considered. First, the defiance must be interfering with the child's ability to function in pre-school, school, home or the community; second, the defiance cannot be the result of another disorder; and third, the child's problem behaviours must be happening for at least six months.

PREVALENCE

There are no figures available for the prevalence of ODD in Ireland, though figures from other countries estimate it affects 2% of all children.

CAUSES

The exact cause of ODD is not known, but it is believed that a combination of biological, genetic and environmental factors may contribute to the condition.

Biological factors: Some studies suggest that defects in or injuries to certain areas of the brain can lead to serious behavioural problems in children. In addition, ODD has been linked to abnormal amounts of chemicals in the brain called neurotransmitters. Neurotransmitters are chemicals that allow messages to be transmitted along the nerve cells or neurons of the body's nervous system. If these chemicals are out of balance or not working properly, messages may not make it through the brain correctly, leading to symptoms of ODD and other mental illnesses. Many children and teenagers with ODD also have other conditions, such as ADHD, learning disorders, depression or an anxiety disorder, which may contribute to their behavioural problems.

Genetic factors: Many children and teenagers with ODD have close family members with either ODD, ADHD or other conditions, including mood disorders, anxiety disorders and personality disorders. This suggests that a tendency to develop ODD may be inherited.

Environmental factors: Factors such as a dysfunctional family life, a family history of mental illnesses and/or substance abuse and inconsistent discipline by parents may contribute to the development of behavioural disorders, although this is certainly not always the case. Many children from perfectly stable homes have ODD.

SYMPTOMS OR CHARACTERISTICS

Symptoms include a pattern of negative, hostile and defiant behaviour lasting at least six months, during which four (or more) of the following are present. (Note: A criterion is met only if the behaviour occurs more frequently than is typically observed in individuals of comparable age and developmental level.)

* Often loses temper, throws repeated temper tantrums.

* Excessively argues with adults.

* Often actively defies or refuses to comply with adults' requests or rules.

* Often deliberately annoys people.

* Often blames others for their own mistakes or misbehaviour.

* Is often easily annoyed by others.

* Is often angry and resentful.

* Swears or uses abusive language.

* Says mean and hurtful things when upset.

For a child's behaviour to be considered indicative of ODD, there must be a significant impairment in social, academic or occupational functioning. Usually in children under six, a diagnosis of ODD will not yet have been made.

SHOW YOU KNOW

Choose one of the below additional needs and write a note on each one under the headings prevalence, causes, symptoms, treatment and the role of the ELC practitioner.

* Attention Deficit and Hyperactivity Disorder (ADHD)

* Oppositional Defiant Disorder

Complex Additional Needs

7.1 INTRODUCTION

Many additional needs affect predominantly one area of development as described in chapters 3–6. Other conditions and syndromes, however, impact on more than one area of development and include:

* Autistic spectrum disorders

* Down syndrome

7.2 AUTISTIC SPECTRUM DISORDERS

Autistic spectrum disorder (ASD) is a term used to describe a group of neurological, developmental disorders which affect how people communicate, socialise and interact with others. It may also be characterised by restrictive, repetitive behaviours, interests and activities.

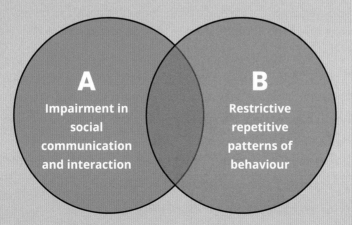

Fig 7.1 Diagnostic criteria for autism DSM-5]

PREVALENCE

The National Council for Special Education (NCSE) collects data on students with ASD with resource teaching support or in special classes and special schools. Their analysis indicates a prevalence rate of 1.55% among children in Ireland. ASD is four times more common in boys.

CAUSES

The cause of autism spectrum disorders is uncertain. Risk factors include having an older parent, a family history of autism and certain genetic conditions. It is estimated that between 64% and 91% of risk is due to family history.

SYMPTOMS OR CHARACTERISTICS

In the past, what we now know as autistic spectrum disorder was divided up into four different disorders, each with its own distinctive set of characteristics. You may still hear the names of these four disorders, which are as follows:

* Autism
* Asperger's syndrome
* Childhood disintegrative disorder
* Pervasive developmental disorder not otherwise specified

Collaborate

In small groups, research one of the four disorders listed above and feed back to the class on what you have found out about each one.

Children with ASD vary considerably in terms of their abilities and skills, e.g. some children with ASD are non-verbal, whereas others have a very sophisticated vocabulary. Children are described as having ASD if they display some or many of the following characteristics:

* A delay in the development of language. Sometimes this delay can be very significant with the child having little or no language even as they progress through their teenage years and into adulthood.
* Delayed toilet training.
* Comprehension difficulties, i.e. may have difficulty understanding direction or instruction.
* Literal thinking and speech, e.g. if someone asks 'What's the story here', the child might reply 'Nobody is telling a story.'
* Poorly modulated intonation and delivery of speech, i.e. speech can sound flat and monotone.
* Echolalia (echoing speech), i.e. repeating what has been said to them.
* Unusual vocabulary, e.g. overly formal use of language.
* Unusual accents or speech patterns, e.g. may speak in accents heard on TV or repeat phrases heard on TV.

* Repetitive use of language, i.e. using the same learned phrases time and time again, e.g. when asked 'How are you?' will use the same answer, for example 'Living the dream', each time.

* Non-verbal difficulties include difficulty in understanding social context, e.g. may speak loudly in church.

* Difficulty empathising with others and appropriately interpreting social cues, e.g. will not understand that others may not share their interest in a topic.

* Unusual body language and facial expressions, e.g. may have little eye contact.

* Gestures are often stiff, stilted or exaggerated.

* Become anxious with changes in routine and have problems with sharing attention, turn-taking and with interactive, imaginative play with others.

* May experience erratic sleep patterns, e.g. some children with ASD sleep very little.

* May display unusual eating habits, e.g. may insist on eating the same foods every day.

* May engage in self-injurious, aggressive or hyperactive behaviour, e.g. head banging or hand biting.

* May engage in repetitive movements such as hand flapping, rocking or spinning.

* May always exhibit an unusual posture or gait, e.g. keeping head down.

* May have irrational fears or phobias.

* May have increased sensitivity to sound, touch, taste or smell.

* May dislike physical contact.

* Very narrow range of interests, e.g. Disney films, and will talk very often about them.

* Some children will show exceptional ability in certain areas.

TREATMENTS AND SUPPORTS FOR CHILDREN WITH ASD

If a parent or guardian thinks that their child may have a disability such as ASD, they can apply under the Disability Act (2005) to the HSE for an Assessment of Need to be carried out. Following the assessment, parents/guardians will receive an Assessment Report stating their child's needs, if any, and the services required to meet those needs. Where a need for supports is identified, a service statement is prepared, which specifies the health services to be provided to the child. Such services may include health professionals such as psychologists, occupational therapists and speech and language therapists. Support can also come from family, friends, other parents/guardians who have children with ASD and from autism support groups.

Extend your learning

The Middletown Centre for Autism in Armagh is a jointly funded initiative between the Department of Education in Northern Ireland and the Department of Education and Skills (DES). The centre provides training for parents and educational professionals about ASD and offers a range of courses. Visit their website for details of upcoming training: www.middletownautism.com.

It is very important for young children with ASD to receive support as early as possible in life to assist their development. The DES has developed a strategy to provide early intervention for children with ASD from the age of two and a half years. Children over three years of age may be enrolled in an autism-specific early intervention class; if such a placement is not available, home tuition may be provided as an interim measure until a school placement is identified. There are also some HSE-funded crèches and pre-school settings.

Children with ASD who are not attending an early intervention class or HSE-funded crèche or pre-school are entitled to a free pre-school place under the ECCE scheme in mainstream crèches and pre-schools. Children with ASD in pre-school are entitled to the same supports whether they are officially diagnosed with ASD or not. Early Years Practitioners can access support for children through the access and inclusion model (AIM), which ensures that children with disabilities can access the ELC programme. Access and inclusion support is applied for by the Early Years' Service, in partnership with the child's parent or guardian. Targeted supports are offered under this scheme that can help the setting better cater for the needs of children with ASD attending the setting. Such supports include:

* In collaboration with the ELC setting the HSE will offer therapeutic supports such as a behaviour support plan to allow practitioners work more effectively with the child.

* Setting may be able to avail of extra funding for minor works, e.g. the installation of a sensory room.

* Settings may be given additional funding for employing extra personnel to help reduce the adult-to-child ratio in the setting.

When a child with ASD reaches school-going age, the available options depend on the child's level of need and where they are geographically located. These provisions include as follows:

* Many children with ASD are educated in mainstream classes in primary and secondary schools, many of whom have additional supports such as a special needs assistant (SNA).

* Special ASD classes attached to mainstream primary and secondary schools are becoming more and more numerous with all counties in Ireland now having a good level of provision.

* Special schools (of which there are 140 in Ireland) cater for children with a wide range of additional needs, including ASD.

Collaborate

Visit the National Council for Special Education website and investigate special classes for children with ASD in primary and secondary schools in your area (click on 'for schools' and then 'special classes' for full list): https://ncse.ie/.

ROLE OF THE ELC PRACTITIONER

Children with a diagnosis of ASD vary enormously in terms of their abilities and challenges so an individual plan must be arrived at in consultation with parents/guardians and any professionals working with the child. However, below are some general strategies that may be useful in an ELC setting:

* Before a child with ASD enrols in an ELC setting, it is vital that practitioners meet with parents/guardians beforehand to get a thorough understanding of the child.

* Children with ASD require a high degree of predictability and routine. It is useful to have the day's routine depicted in pictorial form.

* It is vital that the child has a key worker who knows them well and has a good understanding of their likes and challenges.

* Facilitate the child to play alone but also structure opportunities for the child to play in pairs or small groups.

* Work with parents/guardians to identify effective rewards and reinforcers.

* Help the child to name their feelings and the feelings of others.

* Use visual prompts to indicate a change in activity.

* Teach social interaction skills using social stories (see next page).

* Teach important social skills such as turn-taking, e.g. with a board game or pretend telephone conversations.

* Refer to the child by name if you wish to gain their attention.

* Sometimes the ELC setting will become overwhelming for a child with ASD. A sensory room or area can be very useful as a place where the child can go to calm their emotions. This may be something that could receive funding under the access and inclusion model described above.

Collaborate

Social stories were first developed in the early 1990s by Carol Gray, an American teacher, to help children with ASD gain a better understanding of various social situations, e.g. how to ask a friend to play. Break into groups to research social stories online and as a group develop one social story for use in your ELC work placement setting.

Playing

 Sometimes I like to play with other kids.

 I can ask them, "Do you want to play with me?"

 If they say "yes", I can play with them. I will have fun.

 If they say "no", it's ok.

 I can ask someone else or play by myself.

7.2 DOWN SYNDROME

Down syndrome is a complex additional need that can impact on several aspects of a child's development. Down syndrome was first diagnosed in 1866 by the English doctor John Langdon Down. He described the symptoms of the condition, but it was not understood to be a chromosomal abnormality until 1959, when Professor Jérôme Lejeune, a Parisian geneticist, discovered the genetic explanation for Down syndrome.

PREVALENCE

On average, Down syndrome appears approximately once in every 700 live births but more frequently as maternal age progresses (see table on next page). It is not known exactly why this is the case, although it is thought to be because an older woman's eggs have been exposed to more toxins over time than a younger woman's. Some women, particularly those over the age of 35, opt to have prenatal diagnostic tests done to detect Down syndrome and other genetic abnormalities during pregnancy, though this practice is controversial.

MATERNAL AGE	RISK
15–19	1 in 1,850
20–25	1 in 1,400
26–30	1 in 800
31–35	1 in 380
36–40	1 in 190
41–45	1 in 110
45+	1 in 30

CAUSES

In 1959, Professor Jérôme Lejeune discovered that Down syndrome occurred as a result of a trisomy (three) of chromosome 21. Normally, every cell of a baby's body (except the sex cells) contains a total of 46 chromosomes: 23 from the mother and 23 from the father. A child with Down syndrome gains an extra chromosome 21, usually from the mother, resulting in them having a total of 47. This extra chromosome in each body cell causes the symptoms of the commonest form of Down syndrome, called standard trisomy. It is the severest form of Down syndrome, occurring in approximately 94% of cases.

Since Lejeune's discovery, other forms of the condition, which are much rarer, have been discovered: translocation (where one parent passes on an abnormal rather than an extra chromosome 21 that contains extra material, but not a full chromosome) and mosaicism (where some cells in the body have the normal 46 chromosomes, while others have 47). Approximately 4% of people with Down syndrome have translocation and 2% have mosaic Down syndrome. Individuals with mosaic Down syndrome may show fewer or less severe symptoms of the condition, depending on what percentage of their body cells have 47 chromosomes.

Trisomy Down syndrome

Mosaic Down syndrome

SYMPTOMS OR CHARACTERISTICS

As stated above, Down syndrome is a complex condition, meaning that its symptoms affect a number of different areas of development.

PHYSICAL CHARACTERISTICS AND CHALLENGES

A child with Down syndrome will have several distinctive physical characteristics such as oblique (slanted) eye fissures with extra skin folds on the inner corner of the eyes and a broad round head and face. Neither characteristic poses any problems for the child. Other common physical characteristics, however, can pose problems, including:

* Poor muscle tone and loose joints, which can cause the child to be prone to dislocations and injuries.

* Protruding tongue due to a small oral cavity and an enlarged tongue, which can pose challenges for learning to speak clearly.

* Prone to ongoing respiratory infections.

* Increased incidence of epilepsy.

* Hearing problems sometimes caused by sensorineural factors, other times by chronic serous otitis media, or glue ear.

* Vision problems.

* Short stature with a tendency towards excessive weight gain.

* People with Down syndrome are more prone to certain conditions and diseases, e.g. thyroid disorder, Alzheimer's and leukaemia.

* Delayed fine motor skills because of short, chubby fingers.

* Delay with gross motor skills, although degree of delay varies, e.g. some children will walk before two years, whereas others will be as old as four years.

EFFECTS ON COGNITIVE DEVELOPMENT

Most individuals with Down syndrome have general learning disabilities in the mild (IQ 50–69) to moderate (IQ 35–49) range, while individuals with mosaic Down syndrome typically score 10 to 30 points higher. This is a considerable range, resulting in individuals with Down syndrome having wide-ranging abilities.

EFFECTS ON LANGUAGE DEVELOPMENT

In terms of language development, children with Down syndrome generally experience speech delay. There is often a larger than normal gap between receptive language (what is understood) and expressive language (what is said). They usually require speech therapy in order to improve their expressive (spoken) language. Many initially use a simple sign language, e.g. Lámh, while learning to speak.

EFFECTS ON SOCIAL AND EMOTIONAL DEVELOPMENT

Generally, children with Down syndrome show good social awareness and understanding and therefore are often aware that they are different from their peers. This can lead to feelings of anger, frustration and sadness. Having said this, some children with Down syndrome do not fully understand some of society's social norms and may, for example, be overly friendly to strangers or people they do not know well. In terms of child protection, this has sometimes put them in a vulnerable position.

TREATMENTS AND SUPPORTS FOR CHILDREN WITH DOWN SYNDROME

Down syndrome is a lifelong condition that impacts all areas of development to a greater or lesser degree. Many of the health issues that frequently accompany Down syndrome can be treated and children should be given every opportunity to learn the skills they require to lead as independent a life as possible.

* Children may attend physiotherapy to improve muscle tone and develop motor skills, which may be delayed.

* Children with congenital heart defects often require surgery.

* As a larger proportion of children with Down syndrome have epilepsy than the general population, many may be on anti-epileptic drugs.

* There is a tendency among children and adults with Down syndrome to gain weight, partially because of their short stature, so it is important to monitor eating and for the child to take regular exercise.

* Children may have to have grommets fitted for chronic serous otitis media (glue ear). If the child's hearing difficulties arise from sensorineural factors, hearing aids may be fitted.

* Many children with Down syndrome will wear glasses.

* Speech therapy will prove useful for many children with Down syndrome to help with expressive speech.

In terms of education, children under school-going age can access a free pre-school place under the ECCE scheme in mainstream crèches and pre-schools. Early Years Practitioners can get support for children through the access and inclusion model (AIM), which ensures that children with disabilities can access the ELC programme. Access and inclusion support is applied for by the Early Years' Service, in partnership with the child's parent or guardian. When the child progresses into school, several options are available to them:

* Enrolment in a mainstream class with the assistance of an SNA.

* Enrolment in a special class within a mainstream school.

* Enrolment in a special school.

Regardless of where the child is enrolled, the focus of their education should be as follows:

* Making progress with their cognitive, speech, language and academic skills, with an emphasis on learning skills that will be useful for the future.

* Becoming as independent as possible in their personal care and social lives.

* Developing a positive self-identity, self-confidence and self-esteem.

* Developing a network of friends, personal relationships and leisure interests.

Collaborate

Research has shown that students with Down syndrome gain academic, social and behavioural advantages from being educated with their typically developing peers in mainstream schools (Buckley *et al.*, 2006). Discuss why you believe that the inclusion model of education is particularly beneficial for children with Down syndrome.

ROLE OF THE ELC PRACTITIONER

Children with a diagnosis of Down syndrome can vary considerably in terms of their abilities and challenges so an individual plan must be arrived at in consultation with parents/guardians and any professionals working with the child. Below are some general strategies that may be useful in an ELC setting:

* Children with additional needs (including Down syndrome) should have an individual care and education plan (see chapter 10 for information on education and care plans).

* Children may require assistance with feeding and toileting beyond that of other children. Provide assistance as required but be careful to allow as much independence as possible.

* Up to 80% of children with Down syndrome have some level of hearing impairment at least some of the time. Seat the child close to you or position yourself near them when speech is important, e.g. while giving instructions or at story time.

* Provide visual material to support the spoken word.

* Ensure that the child's hearing aid is working properly and report any concerns about this to their parent/guardian.

* Both receptive and expressive language can be challenging for a child with Down syndrome. When talking to the child, use short, simple sentences, supplementing with visual clues where possible.

* Younger children with Down syndrome use PECS or Lámh while they are learning to speak. It is important for ELC practitioners to become familiar with both of these communication systems.

* Give only simple instructions and allow plenty of time for processing.

* Children with Down syndrome need opportunities to practise and overlearn new skills. Allow time for this.

* Many children with Down syndrome, even while wearing corrective glasses, have difficulty with vision. Use enlarged print books with bold, high-contrast pictures.

* Children with Down syndrome may experience difficulties with fine motor skills. Using a marker pen instead of a pencil for drawing and writing can be helpful as the child does not have to maintain downward pressure. Encourage mark-making and drawing using different mediums, e.g. whiteboard and markers, chalkboard and chalk, wet sand, big crayons. The use of a laptop should be facilitated as the child gets older.

* Children with Down syndrome can tire easily. Watch out for signs that the child is tired and provide nap opportunities for them.

* Keep excellent lines of communication open between the setting and home, using a care diary and, later, a communications journal.

Extend your learning

The Department of Special Education at Mary Immaculate College, Limerick and the Special Educational Support Service have produced a book called *STRANDS*. It is written for educational professionals working with children with intellectual disabilities, including children with Down syndrome.

SHOW YOU KNOW

Choose either ASD or Down syndrome and write a note on it under the headings prevalence, causes, symptoms, treatment and supports and the role of the ELC practitioner.

Section 2

Rights, Legislation and Best Practice

History of Additional Needs Provision in Ireland

8

What I will learn

* The history of additional needs provision in Ireland.

8.1 INTRODUCTION

Swan (2000) described the progression of the education of children with additional needs in Ireland in three phases: the era of neglect and denial, the era of the special school and the era of integration and inclusion.

8.2 THE ERA OF NEGLECT AND DENIAL

Under English rule, the National Education System was established in 1831, making school attendance compulsory for all children between the ages of six and 14. By 1892, children had to attend at least 150 days of school each year (today, the primary school year is 183 days). The government did not consider that the education of children with additional needs was necessary in that their needs were seen as purely medical. Many children with additional needs lived in hospitals, asylums and county homes. However, some religious-run special schools were established at this time. For example, St Mary's School for Deaf Girls in Cabra, Dublin, was established in 1846 by the Dominican order, St Joseph's School for Deaf Boys in Cabra was established in 1857 by the Christian Brothers and St Joseph's School for the Blind was established by the Carmelite order in 1884 in Drumcondra, Dublin. Children from all over the country boarded in these schools from an early age.

From the foundation of the state in 1919 to the early 1990s, practically all education and care, including the education and care of children with additional needs, was carried out by the religious orders in Ireland. As a result, there was little government policy or legislation regarding additional needs provision in Ireland. The situation remained largely the same until the numbers of religious in Ireland began to decline rapidly and many of the schools and institutions formally run by them were taken over by the state. This, together with an increasing awareness among parents, teachers and other professionals of how our additional needs provision had fallen badly behind that of other nations, resulted in a relatively rapid change in government policy and the introduction of several new important pieces of legislation.

8.3 THE ERA OF THE SPECIAL SCHOOL

In 1947, St Vincent's Home for Mentally Defective Children (founded in 1926) was recognised by the state as an official school. The establishment of this school, along with other similar schools that followed, reflected the belief at the time that children with additional needs should not be educated alongside their peers, as this was considered to be detrimental to the education of 'normal' children and their teachers (Commission of Inquiry into the Reformatory and Industrial School System 1934–36). Most children with additional needs at this time were assessed in what were known as County Clinics. After assessment, options were generally limited to institutional care or some form of basic training. In 1959, the first inspector for special education was established, and throughout the 1960s, 1970s and until the mid-1980s, considerable numbers of new special schools were established throughout the state to cater for children with physical, intellectual and sensory disabilities. This was the era of the special school, where it was recognised that children with additional needs required education, but not within the mainstream setting. There are currently 140 special schools providing specialist education for approximately 8,000 pupils annually with over 1,400 teachers teaching in these schools.

8.4 THE ERA OF INTEGRATION AND INCLUSION

In the mid-1980s there was a worldwide lobby for the integration of children with additional needs into mainstream schools. This lobby began to influence Irish educational policy and several classes for children with additional needs were established within mainstream schools; additional resources began to be provided to these schools to support children with additional needs in mainstream classes. Additional needs education became part of teacher training courses in the state's colleges and universities.

In 1991, the government commissioned a comprehensive review of all additional needs provision in Ireland from pre-school through to secondary. On foot of this review, the Report of the Special Education Review Committee (SERC) was published in 1993. In charting a way forward, the review committee proposed seven guiding principles for the education of children with additional needs.

* **Principle 1:** All children, including those with additional needs, have the right to an appropriate education.

* **Principle 2:** The needs of the individual child should be of paramount consideration when decisions are being made concerning the provision of education for children with additional needs.

* **Principle 3:** Parent or guardians are entitled and should be enabled to play an active part in the decision-making process and their wishes taken into consideration.

* **Principle 4:** A continuum of services should be provided ranging from full-time education in mainstream schools to full-time education in special schools.

* **Principle 5:** Except where individual circumstances make it impractical, all children with additional needs should be educated in mainstream schools.

* **Principle 6:** Only in exceptional circumstances should a child have to live away from home to avail of their education.

* **Principle 7:** Adequate resources should be provided to ensure that children with additional needs can have an education appropriate to those needs.

The Education for Persons with Special Educational Needs (EPSEN) Act, 2004 states that a child with special educational needs shall be educated in an inclusive environment with children who do not have such needs unless the nature or degree of those needs is such that to do so would be inconsistent with the best interests of the child or the effective provision of education for children with whom the child is to be educated. This Act resulted in several additional supports being introduced or increased in mainstream schools:

* Employment of Special Needs Assistants.

* Additional allocation of learning support and resource teaching hours.

* Increased allocation of assistive technology.

* School transport and escort service for children with additional needs.

* The establishment of the National Educational Psychological Service in 1999 for educational assessment and planning.

Today in mainstream primary and secondary schools, children with additional needs may be educated fully in mainstream classrooms with additional supports, in a special class within a mainstream school or in a combined model of provision whereby the child attends some of their lessons in mainstream classes and some within a special class.

Today there are a total of 2,034 special classes based in mainstream primary and secondary schools in Ireland catering for children with a range of additional needs including autistic spectrum disorder (ASD), general learning disabilities, specific speech and language disorder, hearing impairment, specific learning disability and multiple disabilities. In addition, there are several ASD early intervention classes for pre-school-aged children attached to mainstream primary schools nationwide.

Extend your learning

Visit the National Council for Special Education website (www.ncse.ie), click on 'for schools' and then 'special classes'. Locate and make a list of the special classes attached to mainstream schools located in your county. Are there any early intervention classes located in your area for pre-school children?

8.5 INCLUSIVE PROVISION IN EARLY YEARS SETTINGS

In the main, early childhood education and care services in Ireland are delivered outside the formal state-funded education system, by a diverse range of private, community and voluntary organisations. Since the implementation of the ECCE scheme in 2010, all children, including those with additional needs, can avail of two free government-funded pre-school years once they turn two years eight months. Where a child has additional needs, the upper age limit of five years six months may be exceeded if required to meet those needs.

When the ECCE scheme was first introduced there was little or no additional support for children with additional needs attending these services. Since the introduction of the access and inclusion model (AIM) in 2016, ELC settings have been able to avail of a range of supports designed to ensure that children with additional needs can access the ECCE programmes. AIM is a child-centred model, involving seven levels of progressive support, moving from the universal to the targeted, based on the needs of the child and the pre-school service. For more information on the access and inclusion model, please see p. 102.

Mainstream ELC settings have had access to a range of supports since the introduction of AIM in 2016 for the education of children with additional needs.

SHOW YOU KNOW

Describe in your own words how additional needs provision in Ireland has progressed from the era of neglect and denial to the era of the special school and finally to the era of integration and inclusion.

9

National and International Legislation, Policy and Regulations

What I will learn

* The important pieces of international and national legislation, policy and regulations that have shaped additional needs provision in Ireland over the past 30 years. This includes:

  * United Nations Convention on the Rights of the Child (1989)
  * Education Act (1998)
  * Child Care Act (1991) and Children Act (2001)
  * Education for Persons with Special Needs Act (2004)
  * Disability Act (2005)
  * Universal Convention on the Rights of Persons with Disabilities (2006)
  * National Quality Framework Síolta (2006)
  * National Curriculum Framework Aistear (2009)
  * Building Regulations Part M (2012)
  * Access and Inclusion Model (2016)
  * Childcare Act 1991 (Early Years Services) Regulations 2016
  * Diversity, Equality and Inclusion Charter (2016)
  * Equal Status Acts 2000–2018
  * First 5 (2019)

9.1 INTRODUCTION

As you saw in chapter 8, the progression of the education and care of children with additional needs in Ireland occurred in three phases: the era of neglect and denial, the era of the special school and the era of integration and inclusion. To a certain extent this progression occurred because of a series of international and national pieces of legislation and government policies and regulations. This chapter shall consider these policies and pieces of legislation with a view to examining how each contributed to the education and care of children with additional needs becoming more accessible and inclusive.

9.2 UNITED NATIONS CONVENTION ON THE RIGHTS OF THE CHILD (1989)

The United Nations Convention on the Rights of the Child (UNCRC) is an internationally binding agreement on the rights of children, adopted by the UN General Assembly in 1989. A child is defined by the UNCRC as a person under the age of 18 years. Ireland signed the convention on 30 September 1990 and ratified it on 28 September 1992. By the ratification, the Irish state committed itself to the promotion, protection and fulfilment of children's rights as outlined by the convention. The convention incorporates children's:

* Civil and political rights (e.g. their treatment under the law).

* Social, economic and cultural rights (e.g. an adequate standard of living).

* Protection rights (e.g. from abuse and exploitation).

The UNCRC sets out children's rights in 54 articles. The convention has several guiding principles, and it is divided into four further core principles: survival, development, protection and participation.

One of the most important guiding principles for children with additional needs is that of non-discrimination (Article 2). The convention applies to all children, whatever their race, religion or abilities, whatever their beliefs are and whatever type of family they come from. It does not matter where they live, what language they speak, whether they are male or female, what their culture is, whether they have a disability or whether they are rich or poor: no child should be treated unfairly on any grounds.

Other articles also have particular importance, especially Article 23 (children with disabilities). Children with a disability of any kind have the right to enjoy a full life and special care and support as well as the other rights set forth in the convention. The child has a right to access education, training, healthcare services, rehabilitation services, preparation for employment and recreation opportunities in a manner conducive to the child achieving the fullest possible social integration and individual development, including his or her cultural and spiritual development.

9.3 EDUCATION ACT (1998)

The Education Act (1998) was the first piece of legislation passed since the foundation of the state that directly outlined the government's rights and legal obligations regarding education. This Act deals primarily, however, with education in primary and secondary school and does not deal specifically with the early childhood education and care sector. While the Act is a general one, encompassing all aspects of education, many parts of it are relevant to additional needs and additional needs education from primary school onwards.

Firstly, the Education Act provided the first legal definition of disability, as follows:

'"Disability" means:

(a) the total or partial loss of a person's bodily or mental functions, including the loss of a part of the person's body, or

(b) the presence in the body of organisms causing, or likely to cause, chronic disease or illness, or

(c) the malfunction, malformation or disfigurement of a part of a person's body, or

(d) a condition or malfunction which results in a person learning differently from a person without the condition or malfunction, or

(e) a condition, illness or disease which affects a person's thought processes, perception of reality, emotions or judgement or which results in disturbed behaviour.' (Part 1, section 2) (See http://www.irishstatutebook.ie/eli/1998/act/51/section/2/enacted/en/html#sec2 for verification)

Secondly, the Act provided the first legal definition of special educational needs: '"Special educational needs" means the educational needs of students who have a disability and the educational needs of exceptionally able students.' (Part 1, section 2)

Thirdly, the Act defines what it means by support services: '"Support services" under the Act include assessments, psychological services, guidance and counselling, access to aids and equipment, transport to and from school, provision of sign language and interpreting services, speech therapy and reasonable accommodations in state examinations.'

This Act has wide-ranging implications for children with additional needs. It recognises their right to participate fully in the life of the school and their right to support and services to allow them to do so. However, the major limitation of this Act is that all the services for children with additional needs mentioned in the Act need only be provided if there is sufficient money to do so. This limits what the government is legally required to provide. This limitation is outlined as follows: '... to provide that, as far as is practicable and having regard to the resources available, there is made available to people resident in the State a level and quality of education appropriate to meeting the needs and abilities of those people.' (Part 2, section 6 (b))

In other words, services should be made available provided there are the resources (money) to do so.

9.4 CHILD CARE ACT (1991)

The legislative basis for dealing with children in need of care and protection is provided by the Child Care Act 1991. The promotion of the welfare of children is the main principle underpinning the Act, together with the protection of children who are at risk of abuse or neglect. The Act puts the onus on the Health Service Executive (HSE), through Tusla, to promote the welfare of children in its area who are not receiving adequate care and protection. The Act recognises that children do best if they can remain with their families, but that the child's safety must always come first. If children are at a real risk of abuse or neglect, it is the role of the HSE (through Tusla) to remove them from their families and care for them elsewhere, e.g. in a foster care environment. The Act is extensive. It is divided into ten parts, each of which deals with a different aspect of child protection.

* **Part 1** gives a short title and defines important terms used throughout the Act, e.g. 'child' means a person under the age of 18 years other than a person who is or has been married.

* **Part 2** outlines the functions of the HSE in relation to child protection, the HSE's duties in relation to homeless children and the functions of childcare advisory committees (these committees help the HSE evaluate how well they are carrying out their functions under the Act).

* **Part 3** deals with the duties of An Garda Síochána to take children to safety and also with emergency care orders where children are taken into care because of immediate risk of harm.

* **Part 4** deals with taking children deemed to be at risk of abuse or neglect into care. The Act explains the regulations regarding interim care orders, care orders and supervision orders. Interim care orders are applied for when it is felt that a child cannot remain where they are while a care order is going through the courts. Interim care orders normally last eight days, although extensions may be granted. Care orders are longer term; they are applied for and last for as long as it is felt necessary. With supervision orders, children are not removed into the care of the HSE but are supervised by HSE personnel. This section of the Act also deals with appeals against care and supervision orders.

* **Part 5** restates the principle underpinning the entire Act – that in all instances, the welfare of the child is paramount. This section also states that the child's wishes should be considered (with consideration for his/her age and level of understanding) in relation to care arrangements. A Guardian ad Litem should be appointed to act on behalf of the child. The section also deals with requests for reports on children and procedures that must be followed if there is a refusal to deliver up a child and they must be searched for under warrant. This section also deals with the media – that certain matters are prohibited from being broadcast or published. This is to protect the identity of the child.

Did you know?

Guardians ad Litem are independent persons appointed by the Court for the duration of Court proceedings relating to a child. They give the child a voice in the proceedings and advise the court in respect of the child's best interests.

* **Part 6** deals with rules and regulations regarding children in care, be it foster care, residential care or in the care of relatives. It also deals with access arrangements for parents/guardians of children in care. The latter part of this section deals with children being adopted while in care together with children leaving care because they have reached 18 years of age and who are going into aftercare. Some children are removed unlawfully from care each year and the Act gives guidance on what should be done in such cases to recover these children.

* **Part 7** deals with pre-school services. Before pre-schools are opened, notification must be given to the HSE. Pre-school services must follow certain operational regulations and the HSE has the power under this Act to inspect pre-school services, demand improvements if necessary and close unsatisfactory services.

* **Part 8** deals with children's residential centres. Children's residential centres must be registered and must closely follow the regulations governing residential centres. If a centre is seen not to be compliant, then it can be removed as a registered centre and not permitted to operate. This decision can be appealed to the district court.

* **Parts 9 and 10** of the Act cover regulations regarding the administration of the Act.

9.5 CHILDREN ACT 2001

Much of the Children Act 2001 relates to children who are young offenders, and while this issue is closely linked to child protection (children who experience neglect and abuse are more likely to become young offenders), this book will focus on Part 2 of the Act, which deals with family welfare conferences. Under the Act, the Children's Court may request a family welfare conference to be convened in respect of a child whom the court feels may be at risk. A chairperson is appointed, and the child's case is investigated. If a child protection issue is found to exist, then a care order or supervision order may be applied for. Several different people may be asked to attend the family welfare conference so that a balanced view of the child's situation is obtained. The child themselves, their parents/guardians, any Guardian ad Litem appointed for the child, other relatives, HSE personnel, ELC or school personnel and any other person who it is felt would make a positive contribution to the conference may be asked to attend. If it is later found that a person attending the conference is not acting with the best interests of the conference and the child in mind, they will be asked to leave. The conference will discuss all the issues relating to the child's welfare and protection and produce a series of recommendations. The Act stipulates that the conference coordinator must notify everyone attending the conference of its recommendations in writing. On receipt of the conference recommendations, the HSE may apply for a care order, supervision order or any other service or support recommended by the conference. Where a conference has been ordered by the Children's Court, the recommendations will also be referred to the court.

Part 3 of the Children Act 2001 makes a specific addition to the Child Care Act 1991 regarding special care orders. These orders are applied for when it is believed that the child poses a substantial risk to their own safety, health, development and welfare because of their own behaviour. This would happen, for instance, if it were found that a child was abusing drugs or alcohol and was at risk of overdose. A special care order could be applied for so that the child could be more closely supervised.

Children with additional needs, particularly if they have intimate physical care needs or difficulty communicating, have been targets for perpetrators of abuse in the past. It is therefore vital that every individual working with children in Ireland in any capacity is familiar with the law in relation to child protection, namely the Child Care Act 1991 and the Children Act 2001 and are also fully aware of *Children First: National Guidance for the Protection and Welfare of Children* (2017). *Children First* is a child protection guidance document for persons working with children and is based on the Childcare Act 1991 and the Children Act 2001 (discussed above). For more information on *Children First*, please see chapter 14, p. 145.

9.6 EDUCATION FOR PERSONS WITH SPECIAL NEEDS ACT (2004)

This is the most significant piece of legislation relating to additional needs in education and comes from the standpoint of **inclusion**. This Act, like the Education Act (1998) described above, relates to a child's education once they enter primary school and does not deal specifically with education in ELC settings. The Act is extensive and covers the following general areas:

* The issue of inclusion with regards to children with additional needs in mainstream settings.

* Preparation of individual education plans for children with additional needs by educational establishments.

* Assessment of additional needs.

* Service provision for children with additional educational needs.

* Appeals.

In relation to inclusion, the Act states that:

'A child with special educational needs shall be educated in an inclusive environment with children who do not have such needs unless the nature or degree of those needs of the child is such that to do so would be inconsistent with:

(a) the best interests of the child as determined in accordance with any assessment carried out under this Act, or

(b) the effective provision of education for children with whom the child is to be educated.' (Section 2)

Under Section 3 of the Act, if the principal of a school believes that a child with additional needs is not making satisfactory progress in the school, they are required to make changes to better address the child's needs. Should no progress still be made, then in consultation with the child's parents, the principal must arrange an assessment to be carried out with the child within one month through the National Council for Special Education (NCSE). After assessment, the NCSE must prepare an **individual education plan (IEP)** for the child. An organiser, called a **special educational needs organiser (SENO)**, helps coordinate the formation of the plan and the school's implementation of it. Depending on the child and their needs, many people may be involved in the formation of the plan – parents, principal, psychologists, speech and language therapists, physiotherapists, child psychiatrists and occupational therapists. There is, therefore, a crossover between the Departments of Health and Education. Should the principal consider that the IEP compiled by the NCSE is unworkable, then through the SENO they can request that a revised plan be compiled. Parents can also appeal plans created for their child if, for example, they feel the plan does not adequately cater for their child's needs, e.g. they feel their child should have a Special Needs Assistant (SNA) and this has not been granted. Parents of children younger than school-going age who suspect their child may have additional needs can arrange for assessment through the HSE. According to the Act (see Section 9), an IEP must include information on the following:

(a) the nature and degree of the child's abilities, skills, and talents

(b) the nature and degree of the child's additional educational needs and how those needs affect their educational development

Each principle is presented using a short statement, followed by an explanation of the principle from the child's perspective. This explanation highlights the adult's role in supporting children's early learning and development. The promotion of the child's uniqueness, equality and diversity are important principles of the Aistear curriculum framework and are concepts that feature throughout the entire framework. Below is an extract from the Aistear framework document.

The child's uniqueness

Each child has his/her own set of experiences and a unique life story. He/she is an active learner growing up as a member of a family and community with particular traditions and ways of life.

- Remember that I am a unique individual with my own strengths, interests, abilities, needs and experiences. Recognise and build on these when you are helping me to learn and develop.
- You know I am a confident and able learner and that I learn at my own rate about things that interest me. Support me to do this in a way that allows me to make decisions about what I learn and when, and how well I am learning.
- I need you, my parents and practitioners, to share what you know about me with each other. By doing this, you can get to know me better and plan things for me to do that will help me to learn in an enjoyable and meaningful way.
- In order for you to understand and support me you need to understand my family background and community. This is especially important if I come from a disadvantaged or marginalised community.

(Aistear, 2009, p. 7)

Equality and Diversity

Nurturing equality and diversity are important in early childhood. Promoting equality is about creating a fairer society in which everyone can participate equally with the opportunity to fulfil his/her potential. Diversity is about welcoming and valuing individual and group differences and understanding and celebrating difference as part of life.

- Support me to feel equal to everyone else and do not let me be excluded because of my special educational need, physical appearance or ability.
- You may have to treat me in a different way to other children, to ensure I feel equal.
- Remember that learning is more meaningful, motivating and enjoyable for me when activities and experiences are based on my skills, strengths and interests and when they are linked to my home culture and language.

(Aistear, 2009, p. 8)

9.11 BUILDING REGULATIONS PART M (2012)

For many years, inaccessible built environments have restricted the ability of individuals with disabilities to participate fully as citizens in Irish society. In the recent past, however, several different Irish policy and legislation documents have been produced and enacted with a view to improving this situation. Part M of the Building Regulations (2012) Access and Use document tries to ensure that buildings are accessible by people with disabilities.

The building regulations apply to the construction of new buildings and extensions to buildings. They also apply when the use of a building is being changed, e.g. from a dwelling house into a pre-school facility. Part M of the regulations tries to ensure that:

* Dwelling houses can be visited by people with disabilities.

* Buildings other than dwellings, e.g. ELC settings, are accessible and usable by people with disabilities.

To satisfy the requirements of the regulations, all buildings should be designed and constructed so that (a) people with disabilities can safely and independently approach and gain access to the building and (b) elements of the building do not create an undue hazard for people with disabilities, including those who are visually impaired.

In addition, non-dwellings should be designed so that (a) people with disabilities can move around within the building and use its facilities, access sanitary accommodation, e.g. toilets, and have access to

A wheelchair user in preschool setting

sufficient suitable spectator seating where applicable, and (b) that there are suitable aids to communication available for people with a visual or auditory impairment.

9.12 ACCESS AND INCLUSION MODEL (2016)

The access and inclusion model (AIM) was first introduced in 2016 as a means of creating a more inclusive environment in pre-schools, so all children, regardless of ability, can benefit from quality early learning and care. This is a welcome development as, before this, most interventions and

supports were available only to children once they reached primary school. The model achieves this by providing universal supports to pre-school settings, and targeted supports that focus on the needs of the individual child, without requiring a diagnosis of disability.

UNIVERSAL SUPPORTS

AIM universal supports benefit all children in the ELC setting by empowering ELC practitioners to create a more inclusive culture in the setting. This is achieved by Continuous Professional Development (CPD).

Examples of CPD opportunities are as follows:

* The Leadership for Inclusion in Early Years Care (LINC) qualification is a Level 6 special purpose award for early years educators hosted by the LINC Consortium which is led by Mary Immaculate College, Limerick and fully funded by the Department of Children, Equality, Disability, Integration and Youth (DCEDIY). With this qualification, pre-school staff can become an Inclusion Coordinator (INCO) in a pre-school setting. Where a service has a fully qualified Inclusion Co-ordinator it will qualify for an increase of €2 per child per week in the rate of ECCE capitation payable.

* The Equality, Diversity and Inclusion (EDI) Charter was developed by DCEDIY to support and empower those working in the ELC sector to explore, understand and develop inclusive practices. EDI training helps providers understand the EDI charter and guidelines and create their own inclusion charter for their setting.

* AIM also supports settings by providing three additional (CPD) courses in the areas of disability and inclusion. These are:

    * **Hanen** – Hanen Teacher Talk is a three-day training course for providers, to help them enable young children to develop language and literacy skills.

    * **Lámh** – Lámh is a manual sign language system used by children and adults with intellectual disability and communication needs.

    * **SPEL** – SPEL stands for Sensory Processing eLearning programme and helps providers support children with sensory processing difficulties.

TARGETED SUPPORTS

For many children, AIM universal supports will be sufficient to ensure inclusion. However, some children may require further supports to ensure that they can participate meaningfully in the ELC programme. Targeted support caters for the needs of the child and does not require a diagnosis of an additional need. Targeted supports available are as follows:

1. **Expert educational advice and support:** this is provided by Better Start Early Years Specialist Service (EYSS). Early Years Specialists work collaboratively with parents, pre-school providers and other professionals to develop inclusive learning environments in pre-schools. The EYSS also provides coaching and mentoring to the pre-school staff supporting children with additional needs in ELC settings. This includes the creation of an Access and Inclusion Plan for children, which can help identify additional support and resources required to meet the needs of the child in the pre-school room. The EYSS can also act as a liaison with the National Council for Special Education to support transitions to primary school.

2. **Equipment, Appliances and Minor Alterations:** specialised equipment, appliances or capital grants towards minor building alterations may be provided as targeted supports to ensure a child's meaningful participation in pre-school. This could include, for example, a hoist, hearing aid or wheelchair ramp. Training in the use of equipment is given to providers free of charge.

3. **Therapy Services:** AIM provides a range of services in collaboration with the HSE under therapeutic supports. Targeted services are individualised and may include supports such as behaviour support plans, classes, equipment, professional advice or pre-school visits. Supports may be provided through a Children's Disability Network Team (CDNT), HSE Disability Service, HSE-funded Voluntary Organisations or HSE Primary Care Services.

4. **Additional Capitation:** AIM may provide additional funding to pre-schools who have a child requiring extra support. Providers can use this funding either to reduce the child-to-adult ratio in the pre-school room or to fund an extra staff member as a shared resource with other children in the setting.

Extend your learning

Visit the Access and Inclusion Model website (aim.gov.ie) to find out how ELC settings can apply for universal and targeted supports.

9.13 CHILDCARE ACT 1991 (EARLY YEARS SERVICES) REGULATIONS 2016

The Childcare Act 1991 (Early Years Services) Regulations 2016 are essentially a set of rules or requirements that came into effect for ELC settings on 30 June 2016. The regulations are divided into nine different parts, each of which deals with a different aspect of ELC provision.

* **Part 1** defines terms used in the Act and regulations, e.g. 'full day-care service' means a pre-school service offering a structured day-care service for pre-school children for more than five hours per day and which may include a sessional pre-school service for pre-school children not attending the full day-care service.

* **Part 2** deals with the regulations and requirements regarding the registration of a pre-school service, e.g. a person wishing to open a pre-school service must make their application at least three months in advance of opening.

* **Part 3** deals with rules and regulations in relation to the management and staffing of pre-school services, e.g. all services must have a designated person in charge and a named person who is able to deputise as required. This part also deals with staffing ratios and staff recruitment procedures.

* **Part 4** deals with the type of records that must be kept on each child and the information that must be provided to parents of children attending the service, e.g. the following information must be obtained and securely retained on each child:

  * Name and date of birth of the child.
  * Date on which the child first attended the service.
  * Date on which the child ceased to attend the service.
  * Contact details of the child's parents/guardian and also emergency contact details of another relative or friend.
  * Authorisation for the collection of the child.
  * Details of any illness, disability, allergy or additional need.
  * Name of the child's GP.
  * Record of immunisations (if any).
  * Written consent for appropriate medical treatment in the event of an emergency.

* **Part 5** deals with the facilities that must be available for the child in relation to rest, play, equipment and materials, food and drink. For example, a registered provider shall ensure that adequate, suitable, nutritious and varied food and drink is available for each pre-school child attending the pre-school service.

* **Part 6** deals with regulations regarding safeguarding the health, safety and welfare of the child, e.g. checking children in and out of the service, first aid, fire safety, supervision and insurance.

* **Part 7** deals with requirements regarding the quality of the building in which the service is provided and minimum space requirements per child. For example, a registered provider of a sessional pre-school service or a pre-school service in a drop-in centre shall ensure that a minimum of 1.818 square metres of clear floor space is available for each child attending the service.

* **Part 8** deals with requirements regarding the reporting of incidents, e.g. the reporting of a serious injury to a pre-school child while attending the service. This part also deals with the procedure that providers must follow in relation to complaints.

* **Part 9** deals with inspection and enforcement. All pre-school services are subject to inspection to ensure their compliance with the Childcare Act 1991 (Early Years Services) Regulations 2016. Failure to comply can result in closure of the service.

The Childcare Act 1991 (Early Years Services) Regulations 2016 also has seven schedules each giving further detail in relation to parts 1–9 above. The schedules are as follows:

* Schedule 1 Application Fees
* Schedule 2 Application Form for Registration of Pre-School Service
* Schedule 3 Application Form for Registration of Temporary Pre-School Service
* Schedule 4 Form for Notification of Change in Circumstances
* Schedule 5 Policies, Procedures and Statements
* Schedule 6 Adult:Child Ratios
* Schedule 7 Minimum Space Requirements

REFLECTIVE PRACTICE

The following policies, procedures and statements are required by the Childcare Act 1991 (Early Years Services) Regulations 2016. Choose one policy, procedure or statement. When you are next on work placement, ask to see your choice.

(a) Statement of purpose and function

(b) Complaints policy

(c) Policy on administration of medication

(d) Policy on infection control

(e) Policy on managing behaviour

(f) Policy on safe sleep

(g) Fire safety policy

(h) Inclusion policy

(i) Outings policy where children attending the service are brought on such outings

(j) Policy on accidents and incidents

(k) Policy on authorisation to collect children

(l) Policy on healthy eating

(m) Policy on outdoor play where such play is provided to children attending the service

(n) Policy on overnight services where the service is an overnight pre-school service

(o) Policy on staff absences

(p) Policy on the use of the internet and photographic and recording devices

(q) Recruitment policy

(r) Risk management policy

(s) Settling-in policy

(t) Staff training policy

(u) Supervision policy

9.14 DIVERSITY, EQUALITY AND INCLUSION CHARTER (2016)

The *Diversity, Equality and Inclusion Charter* and its accompanying guidelines was published by the Department of Children and Youth Affairs in 2016. The 100-page document is divided into two parts:

* Part A: Early childhood care and education national inclusion charter.

* Part B: Diversity, equality and inclusion guidelines.

Part A offers a vision of what diversity, equality and inclusion looks like in ELC settings.

The principles of inclusion, from the Diversity, Equality and Inclusion charter

Part B offers guidelines for how to achieve this vision. This part of the document is divided into five sections.

1. Understanding diversity, equality and inclusion.

2. Diversity, equality and inclusion – developing an anti-bias approach.

3. Diversity, equality and inclusion – physical environment.

4. Diversity, equality and inclusion – supporting families.

5. Developing and implementing an inclusion policy.

UNDERSTANDING DIVERSITY, EQUALITY AND INCLUSION

In this section the emphasis is on using the correct language and terminology when speaking about diversity, equality and inclusion.

DIVERSITY, EQUALITY AND INCLUSION – DEVELOPING AN ANTI-BIAS APPROACH

In this section the emphasis is on the concept of anti-bias. Anti-bias is concerned with avoiding and challenging prejudice, i.e. avoiding and challenging false beliefs about individuals or groups based on their gender, marital status, family status, age, disability, sexual orientation, race, religion or ethnic background. This section offers direction on how to achieve this.

DIVERSITY, EQUALITY AND INCLUSION – PHYSICAL ENVIRONMENT

In this section guidance is given on how to ensure that the physical environment in ELC settings does not pose a barrier to accessibility, diversity or inclusion, e.g. the layout of the setting should not pose a difficulty for a child with a physical disability.

DIVERSITY, EQUALITY AND INCLUSION – SUPPORTING FAMILIES

In this section the emphasis is on working in partnership with parents and guardians. It recognises that parents and guardians know their children best and that open and frequent communication is essential.

DEVELOPING AND IMPLEMENTING AN INCLUSION POLICY

This section gives guidance to ELC settings on how to develop an inclusion policy. It provides an inclusion policy template for settings to use to create a policy suited to their own needs.

Collaborate

Download and print the Diversity, Equality and Inclusion Charter (2016). In groups, take one of the five parts of the guidelines; each group then summarises a part. Nominate one person from each group to present their section to the class.

9.15 EQUAL STATUS ACTS 2000–2018

The Equal Status Act was first enacted in 2000. Since then, several amendments have been made. This Act is now referred to as the Equal Status Acts 2000–2018. These Acts prohibit discrimination on eleven different grounds (the original Act had nine):

1. Gender – male, female or transgender.
2. Civil status – married, single, separated, divorced or widowed.
3. Family status – being a parent/guardian to a child under 18 or being the primary carer to a person over 18.
4. Sexual orientation – heterosexual, bisexual or homosexual.
5. Religion.
6. Age.
7. Disability.
8. Race.
9. Traveller community.
10. Housing assistance – persons in receipt of housing supplement.
11. Victimisation – a person who has sought redress, attended as a witness or opposed an unlawful act.

* Difficulty playing in a cooperative manner.

* Difficulty sharing.

* Difficulty speaking or understanding speech/language.

* Physical development issues, e.g. difficulties standing, walking, holding a pencil, picking up items or coordination due to poor gross and fine motor skills.

In early years settings the access and inclusion model (AIM) provides a range of universal and targeted supports to provide early intervention for children with additional needs (see also chapter 9).

10.4 INDIVIDUAL EDUCATION PLANS (IEPS)

The Education for Persons with Special Educational Needs (EPSEN) Act was published in Ireland in 2004. One of the key provisions of the Act was to provide the legislative basis for the introduction of individual education plans (IEPs) for children with additional needs in primary and secondary schools. It is good practice in ELC settings to have individual education and learning plans for all children, but particularly children with additional needs. An IEP is a written plan prepared for a named child. It is a record of what is being agreed as 'additional to' and 'different from' the usual differentiated curriculum provision that is provided to all children in the setting. Plans should be created in consultation with parents/guardians and any other professionals working with the child, e.g. speech and language therapists. Plans for young children should be short term in nature and reviewed and evaluated regularly. IEPs are working documents to be added to, amended and updated as appropriate, depending on the individual needs of the child. IEPs must contain key information, including:

* The child's strengths and needs.

* The child's current level of development established through child observations.

* Specific targets for the child.

* Success criteria.

* Details of the strategies and resources required to achieve targets.

* Date of review of plan.

10.5 APPROPRIATE LANGUAGE

When writing or speaking about people with additional needs it is important to put the person first, e.g. child with autism. Phrases such as 'the blind', 'the deaf' or 'the disabled' do not reflect the people's individuality, equality or dignity. The National Disability Authority recommends that the following terms be used:

* Term no longer in use: the disabled
  Term now used: person with a disability

* Term no longer in use: wheelchair-bound or confined to a wheelchair
  Term now used: wheelchair user

* Term no longer in use: cripple, spastic
  Term now used: person with a disability

* Term no longer in use: the handicapped
  Term now used: disabled person, person with a disability

* Term no longer in use: mental handicap
  Term now used: intellectual disability

* Term no longer in use: mentally handicapped
  Term now used: intellectually disabled

* Term no longer in use: normal
  Term now used: non-disabled

* Term no longer in use: suffers from (e.g. asthma)
  Term now used: has (e.g. asthma)

10.6 ADOPTING AN INCLUSIVE APPROACH

Adopting an inclusive approach means recognising the differences between children and using this knowledge to design and adapt the curriculum offered in the setting to ensure that all children can access it and participate fully in their learning. The Diversity, Equality and Inclusion Charter and its accompanying guidelines recommend that all settings have an inclusion policy that indicates to practitioners how settings may be made more inclusive. When planning activities for children, practitioners must always consider how this activity may need to be adapted to make it accessible to children with additional needs in the setting, e.g. seating a

Inclusion in the pre-school setting

child with a hearing impairment close to you at story time so that they can see the illustrations to help aid their understanding. Inclusion also means promoting social relationships and friendships among all children in the setting and giving each child a sense of identity and belonging.

10.7 VALUING INDIVIDUALITY

The concept of individuality is closely related to the topics of inclusion and individual education planning as described above. Individuality in an ELC means recognising each child's unique strengths and interests, and also their unique challenges. Valuing individuality involves observing each child closely to find ways of responding to these unique strengths, interests and challenges and adapting the curriculum offered accordingly.

REFLECTIVE PRACTICE

Adrian is a four-year-old child with autism. He has a very keen interest in dinosaurs with an almost encyclopaedic knowledge of them. Adrian finds it challenging to interact with the other children and spends a lot of time working on his own. Think of ways in which you as an ELC practitioner could use Adrian's interest in dinosaurs to help him relate to other children in the setting.

10.8 ACCESS

Access, when speaking about children with additional needs, can mean both the physical adaptation of the setting and the adaptation of the curriculum offered there to meet the additional needs of children attending. Until the introduction of the access and inclusion model in 2016, ELC settings were offered little support in making settings accessible to children with additional needs. The access and inclusion model, as you read in chapter 9, offers both universal and targeted supports to settings to help them meet the needs of all children in the setting, including those with additional needs (see page 102).

10.9 ADVOCACY

When working with a child with additional needs, advocacy means being the main point of contact for the child and their parents/guardians. The role of an advocate in an ELC setting is to liaise between the child, their parents/guardians and other practitioners in the setting. Advocates also support children and their families by giving them a voice in relation to the education and care offered to them. In ELC settings, an advocate is usually also the child's key worker. They will be involved in the development of the child's IEP and will coordinate communication between the setting and the child's home and vice versa.

10.10 EMPOWERMENT

Empowerment means involving children in the decisions that affect them, appropriate to their age and level of understanding. Giving children choices about the activities they want to get involved in is one example of how adults can promote empowerment. Children also feel empowered when permitted to do things for themselves. It is important that adults observe what children can do by themselves to give them as much independence as possible.

Example of empowerment: a baby self-feeding

An example of empowerment is allowing young children to self-feed under careful adult supervision. With older children, having a mealtime routine whereby they set the table and clear away afterwards and have a choice of snacks and drinks to choose from are examples of promoting empowerment. Empowering young children has many advantages. It increases self-esteem and self-confidence; it promotes independence and an increased interest in learning as children are more likely to engage in activities that they themselves have chosen to partake in.

10.11 CONFIDENTIALITY

As an acknowledgement of the rights of the child and their family, any information gathered while working with children with additional needs and their families in ELC settings must be treated in the strictest confidence and not shared with people outside the setting. Information such as professional reports, assessments or

Confidential record keeping is a principle of good practice of working with children with additional needs

observations should be kept in a secure location, usually in a locked cabinet in a central office or digitally on an internal password-protected computer system.

10.12 INDEPENDENCE

One of the important concepts that parents/guardians and practitioners working with children with additional needs must be acutely aware of is that of independence. Adults working with the child can become overprotective of that child in an effort to help them maximise their potential and help them to avoid difficulties. It is vital, however, to give the child as much independence as possible to help them build up their own confidence and realise just how much they can do on their own. One way of starting to build independence is by giving the child a choice so that they are in more control of their day. Choice also promotes empowerment (discussed above) and allows the child to advocate for themselves. Adults should avoid 'doing things' for children (including those with additional needs) that they are capable of doing for themselves. The child's efforts may not be perfect and may take more time, but if you learn to stand back, offering support only if asked, it gives the child opportunities to practise and improve their skills as well as a sense of achievement and pride.

To promote independence, observe the child and provide challenges for them that you judge they can achieve with effort and practice. This allows the child to see just how much they can achieve when they put their mind to it. If certain tasks are too difficult for them, consider how tasks could be adapted to their current abilities.

Use assistive technology and devices where appropriate, e.g. use of a PECS board to allow children with additional communication needs to communicate their choices.

10.13 BOUNDARIES

In caring professions such as ELC, social work or healthcare, there are lines drawn between professional and personal relationships that are referred to as professional boundaries. Professional boundaries help differentiate between actions that are professionally appropriate and those that are inappropriate or unprofessional. Professional relationships can appear quite differently in early childhood settings than they do in other caring professions. Unlike other professions, early childhood educators have a particularly intimate relationship with families. They may be with children longer and more often, sometimes as many as 40 hours a week. They have close, affectionate and physical interactions with children, including caring for children's most intimate physical needs. They have sensitive information about a child's development and about the life of the family, including details about relationships between family members and their child or about the household's financial situation.

Additionally, it is not uncommon, especially in smaller communities, for practitioners to have more than one kind of relationship with a family. For example, a practitioner may play on the same sports team as a parent, or they may be relatives or have grown up together. When practitioners have a dual relationship (a personal connection outside the professional role) with a family member, awareness of professional boundaries becomes especially important.

Boundary crossings occur when professional lines of behaviour are crossed that may be inadvertent, thoughtless or even a purposeful attempt to meet the needs of a child or family. They are non-exploitative. Boundary violations, on the other hand, are exploitative or potentially harmful to children and families.

Examples of boundary crossings include:

* Socialising with the family of an enrolled child.
* Seeking favours, e.g. asking a parent for professional advice.
* Disclosing personal information about yourself, e.g. sharing personal problems.
* Giving advice beyond the scope of your role, e.g. offering marital advice.
* Breaching confidentiality, e.g. talking about a child's issues outside the work setting.

Examples of boundary violations include:

* Showing favouritism or bias towards a child and their family.
* Accepting gifts or favours.
* Engaging in an intimate relationship, e.g. dating the parent of an enrolled child.

10.14 CHILD PROTECTION

Child protection will be dealt with in chapter 14 (see page 145).

10.15 TERMINOLOGY USED WHEN WORKING WITH CHILDREN WITH ADDITIONAL NEEDS

When working with children with additional needs, certain terminology and phrases are used and need to be fully understood. The following terms will be explained in this section: equality, diversity, discrimination and stereotyping.

EQUALITY

Principle 5 of Síolta concerns the issue of equality. As explained in both Article 2 of the UN Convention on the Rights of the Child (1989) and the Equal Status Acts (2000, 2004), equality is a fundamental right and should be a fundamental characteristic of quality early childhood education and care. Equality does not mean treating all children the same. It instead involves recognising the needs and abilities of each individual child and adapting the service provided to each one so that all children can access what is on offer equally.

DIVERSITY

Principle 6 of Síolta concerns the issue of diversity. The term 'diversity' is used to describe differences in individuals in terms of their gender, age, skin colour, language, sexual orientation, ethnicity, ability, religion, race or other background factors, such as family structure or economic circumstances. Quality settings recognise, respect and celebrate diversity, e.g. by educating children about unfamiliar cultures and traditions.

DISCRIMINATION

The term 'discrimination' is used to describe unjust or prejudicial treatment of different categories of people, e.g. on the grounds of race, age, sex or disability.

STEREOTYPING

Stereotyping occurs when an individual or group has a generalised and prejudiced view of another individual or group. Stereotypes are frequently inaccurate, and are resistant to new information. In relation to working with children with additional needs, to avoid stereotyping it is important to always view the child as an individual with their own strengths, interests and needs.

SHOW YOU KNOW

Choose three of the principles of good practice for working children with additional needs listed below and, in your own words, write a short account of each.

* Respecting parents/guardians as partners
* Early intervention
* Individual Education Plans
* Appropriate language
* Adopting an inclusive approach
* Valuing individuality
* Access
* Advocacy
* Empowerment
* Confidentiality
* Independence
* Boundaries
* Child protection

Section 3

Accessible and Inclusive Experiences

Making Learning Experiences Relevant and Meaningful, and Barriers to Participation

What I will learn

* How to make learning relevant using the Aistear framework.
* The benefits of relevant, meaningful learning experiences to children's growth and development.
* Barriers to participation.

11.1 INTRODUCTION

Principle 10 of the Aistear curriculum framework is titled 'Relevant and Meaningful Experiences'. Aistear states that:

'Relevant and meaningful experiences make learning more enjoyable and positive for children. On-going assessment of what children do, say and make, and reflection on these experiences helps practitioners to plan more developmentally appropriate and meaningful learning experiences for children. This also enables them to improve their practice. Assessment is about building a picture of children's individual strengths, interests, abilities and needs and using this to support and plan for their future learning and development.'

(Aistear, 2009, p. 11)

This chapter shall focus on how practitioners can make experiences more relevant and meaningful for children, especially those with additional needs, and the benefits that this practice has for the child.

11.2 MAKING LEARNING RELEVANT AND MEANINGFUL

CONNECT TO PRIOR LEARNING

Children learn best if what they are learning is connected in some way to what they already know. This idea is based around constructivist theories of development such as those proposed by Jean Piaget (1896–1980). In practice, this means planning activities that connect with the child's previous experiences while at the same time challenging the child to extend their knowledge and skills.

Example

When talking about the climate in different countries around the world, a group of pre-school children are asked to talk about whether they have ever visited another country on holiday and what the weather was like in that country. The children then look at a large map of the world and are helped to find the countries they have visited. The ELC practitioner explains to the children what the equator is and that the closer a country is to the equator the hotter the weather will be. Using a ruler, the children measure how close the country they have visited is to the equator and then compare it to Ireland.

DEVELOPMENTALLY APPROPRIATE

The importance of presenting experiences and activities to children that are developmentally appropriate is based on the work of Lev Vygotsky (1896–1934) and his concept of the zone of proximal development. The zone of proximal development (ZPD) is the area between what a child can do on their own and what they can do with adult or more able peer assistance. Tasks that children can just about master alone are at the very bottom of their ZPD and those they can master only with assistance are at the top. Tasks that are too easy or too difficult for the child are outside the zone altogether and will provide little interest for them or may, indeed, cause frustration. Vygotsky believed that teaching is about finding each child's ZPD and guiding them along it. Tasks outside the zone – too easy (below) or too difficult (above) – should not be presented, as children will quickly become either bored and uninterested or frustrated and give up. In ELC settings, practitioners use child observations to assess where the child is in terms of their development. They then plan activities and experiences based on these observations.

EMERGING INTERESTS

Both Aistear and Síolta advocate the development of an emerging interest and inquiry-based curriculum. When this type of curriculum is provided it evolves as choices and connections are made by the children as they discover the world around them. There is an emphasis on child-led learning. This type of curriculum builds on the interests of both the children and practitioners. Sometimes experiences and activities emerge from children's interests and at other times from practitioners.

Example

Penny is a four-year-old girl with Down syndrome. She has recently returned from a holiday with her parents in Spain and has brought in some photographs from the holiday. She is very excited to tell everyone about the experience. Bella, the room leader, uses Penny's photographs to begin a topic where the children learn about Spain.

EQUALITY OF OPPORTUNITY

When working with children with additional needs in ELC settings, equality of opportunity is not about providing the same opportunities to all children in terms of the learning experiences being offered to them. It is instead about using observation to work out children's needs, interests, abilities and challenges, and devising activities and experiences designed to meet those needs and interests.

11.3 BENEFITS OF RELEVANT AND MEANINGFUL EXPERIENCES

INCREASED MOTIVATION, INTEREST AND ENGAGEMENT

When children are presented with a curriculum that is developmentally appropriate to their age and stage of development, is based on their emerging interests and connected to what they already know, motivation, interest and engagement levels increase.

INCREASED CONFIDENCE AND SELF-ESTEEM

Children respond positively in a learning environment where they can choose what activities they engage with. When the learning environment is too adult-led children are less likely to take ownership of their own learning and may begin to disengage. This can negatively impact

Children absorbed in pre-school activity

children's confidence and self-esteem. In addition, where there is a 'one size fits all' approach to the experiences and activities presented to children, some may struggle and begin to doubt their own abilities. This can be particularly true for children with additional needs. Through careful observation, ELC practitioners learn what interests individual children and plan a learning environment appropriate to their needs and abilities.

TAKING RESPONSIBILITY FOR THEIR OWN LEARNING

During the first five years of life in particular, children's learning and development progresses at an incredible rate. They learn a vast range of skills with little direct instruction, taking responsibility for their own learning. As children progress through pre-school, primary and secondary school, however, many begin to take less and less responsibility for their own learning. The educationist John Caldwell Holt (1923–1985) believed this was because teaching becomes more and more adult-led as time goes on and children begin to disengage from learning. To prevent this from happening, activities and experiences presented in ELC settings should be child-led and child-centred. This can be done by providing a wide range of learning resources for children and giving them choice in how they interact with them.

Extend your learning

After several years of teaching in the American elementary school system, John Holt became very disillusioned with it and became an advocate of home schooling. Research and find out what problems Holt saw with the education system and why he believed it was causing most children to fail to reach their full potential.

11.4 BARRIERS TO PARTICIPATION

ACCESS

Lack of access can act as a barrier to participation by children with additional needs, their parents/guardians or the practitioners working with them, and can take several forms.

Physical access: children with additional physical needs can experience problems if settings are not physically accessible. The buildings regulations Part M (2012) has done a lot to alleviate this issue; however, this barrier to participation can be experienced where settings were established prior to the introduction of these regulations.

Access to the curriculum: up until the introduction of the access and inclusion model (AIM) in 2016, ELC settings were given little support to assist with the inclusion of children with additional needs into their settings. ELC practitioners had limited access to continuous professional development (CPD) to gain additional knowledge and skills. The AIM model has been in operation for only a relatively short time and it therefore remains to be seen how effective it will be.

Access to useful knowledge: assessment reports developed and created by psychologists and other professionals can often be inaccessible to practitioners on the ground. Most reports offer a recommendations section, but should be tailored more toward giving practical accessible advice and tips to the adults working with the child on a daily basis.

LANGUAGE

Language can act as a barrier to participation in several different ways:

* Children with particular additional needs, such as hearing impairment, specific speech and language impairment or children whose first language is not that of the setting can experience challenges accessing the curriculum provided by the setting.

* Parents/guardians with a hearing impairment, whose first language is not that of the setting or who have dyslexia may experience difficulties communicating with the setting, e.g. communicating with practitioners or understanding information sent home.

* The language used by professionals such as psychologists and others can be inaccessible to parents/guardians and, indeed, ELC professionals, thus creating a barrier to understanding the needs of the child and how those needs can best be met.

ATTITUDES AND BIAS

Working effectively with children with additional needs requires additional planning and resources. Settings and practitioners must therefore have a very positive and progressive attitude if they are to provide a quality service. Additional training must often be undertaken, and time given to planning and applying for extra resources and supports. Settings must be very committed to this aspect of provision for it to meet the needs of the children with additional needs. ELC services in Ireland are largely private companies and are not currently given the government-funded supports offered to primary and secondary schools, e.g. access to special needs assistants. This can act as a barrier to participation.

LACK OF UNDERSTANDING AND AWARENESS

Until recently, the education and care of children with additional needs was not a compulsory part of ELC practitioner training, certainly at QQI Levels 5 and 6. This may have led to a lack of understanding and awareness among practitioners. Since the launch of AIM (2016), practitioners working in the sector now have access to free additional training in this area and from 2021 the education and care of children with additional needs is a compulsory part of ELC training.

GOVERNMENT FUNDING

Unlike some other countries such as Sweden and Germany, ELC is not fully state funded in Ireland but is instead provided by private companies. The ECCE scheme, first introduced in 2010, provides some financial support to families wishing to avail of ELC services but this is still considered inadequate. Current funding models in the ELC sector make it exceedingly difficult for service providers to attract and retain well-qualified and experienced staff. ELC settings do not have access to the supports available in primary and secondary school settings, such as special education needs organisers, psychologists, special needs assistants and special needs coordinators. AIM (2016) has sought to address this issue. It is too early to say what impact this initiative will have on provision of a high-quality service for children with additional needs in ELC settings.

FINANCIAL CONSTRAINTS ON PARENTS/GUARDIANS

According to a recent UNICEF report, Ireland ranks among the world's most expensive countries for childcare, with families spending half of their salaries, on average, for the service. The ECCE scheme, mentioned above, provides some support but is limited to 76 weeks over two years and does not provide an all-day service for parents/guardians who are working full-time.

SHOW YOU KNOW

* Describe two ways the Aistear framework suggests practitioners can make learning relevant and meaningful in ELC settings.
* Explain two benefits of relevant, meaningful learning experiences to children's growth and development.
* Name and describe two barriers to participation that can be experienced by children with additional needs and/or their parents or guardians.

Specialist Aids and Equipment

12.1 INTRODUCTION

This chapter will focus on the range of specialist aids and equipment available to children with additional needs to help them participate fully in the activities and experiences being offered in the ELC setting. In many cases, the child will already have been assessed by their healthcare professionals and will already be using their specialist aids or equipment upon entry to the setting. In other cases, settings may identify specific pieces of equipment that the child does not already have access to and apply for funding under the access and inclusion model (AIM) 2016 (targeted supports).

12.2 SPECIALIST AIDS AND EQUIPMENT FOR CHILDREN WITH ADDITIONAL PHYSICAL NEEDS

MOBILITY AIDS

There are numerous mobility aids, also called assistive technologies or assistive devices, to help with the mobility limitations associated with additional needs such as cerebral palsy and spina bifida. Assistive devices will be adjusted to fit the child's height or can be specially made to fit their individual needs. The type of device used will depend on the child's individual mobility needs. Assistive devices greatly improve the child's quality of life by increasing their independence.

A child with leg braces supporting the foot and ankle

* **Orthotic devices** are braces worn externally that improve and strengthen mobility. There are several different types of brace: some may support only the foot and ankle, while others may support the foot, ankle, knees and hips.

* **Walkers** can assist children with their mobility issues, including problems with balance and posture. They also allow the child to bear weight on their legs, which increases bone strength and reduces the risk of fractures and osteoporosis in later life.

For a child with mobility issues, a walker improves their quality of life by increasing their independence but also increases their bone strength.

* **Crutches** are often used by children with mobility issues who can ambulate, or walk, but need extra help with balance and stability. There are two types of crutch, i.e. underarm or forearm.

A child using forearm crutches

* **Standers** are devices that allow children with additional needs such as cerebral palsy to stand for short or extended periods of time. They help to support the child's weight and provide stability while in the upright position.

A child with cerebral palsy using a stander

* **Wheelchairs** are common mobility aids for children with greater mobility needs. There are numerous design options and features to choose from, but there are two basic types: manual wheelchairs and power, or electric, wheelchairs. Manual wheelchairs must be propelled by the user or pushed by another person, while power wheelchairs are motorised. Special paediatric wheelchairs are available for younger children.

A paediatric wheelchair propelled by the user

* **Specialist seating** is available for children who need additional support while eating or doing tabletop activities.

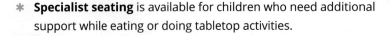

An example of specialist seating

* **Support wedges** give the child support while engaged in floor play.

Support wedges

FEEDING AIDS

* **Specialist cutlery** is useful to help children who may find standard cutlery difficult to use or control. Children's cutlery sets are available with contoured handles in bright colours. The handles of this cutlery are normally wider and may be curved. This makes it more comfortable in the child's hand, as well as being easier to control than standard narrow cutlery, helping the child develop the skills they need to feed themselves independently.

Children's cutlery

* **Specialist plates and bowls** are available for children who may find it challenging to use standard products. Suction or non-slip bases are key components in many of these products. Children with motor-control issues may have difficulty holding bowls in place on hard tables.

Example of a specialist plate with a non-slip base

* **Drinking cups** are available that are non-spill and are easy to grip and drink from.

A non-spill drinking cup

WRITING AIDS

* **Pencil grips** can be put on standard pens and pencils to increase their diameter and make them easier to use.

Pencil grips

* **Slanted writing boards** allow children with additional needs such as dysgraphia and dyspraxia to write more easily. Specialist paper is also available where the lines are slightly raised, helping the child to control the size of the letters they are forming.

Raised lined paper

127

12.3 SPECIALIST AIDS AND EQUIPMENT FOR CHILDREN WITH ADDITIONAL LANGUAGE AND COMMUNICATION NEEDS

HEARING IMPAIRMENT

As you learned in chapter 5, there is a range of hearing aids available for children with hearing impairment.

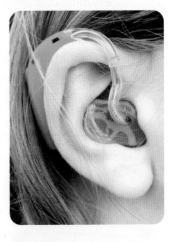

*   **Behind-the-ear hearing aids (BTE)**, as the name suggests, are worn behind the ear and are connected to a custom-made silicone or acrylic ear mould that fits inside the outer ear.

A behind-the-ear hearing aid with a silicone ear mould

A behind-the-ear open-fitting hearing aid

*   **Behind-the-ear open-fitting hearing aids** are used if a child's hearing loss is in the mild to moderate range. This still includes a BTE aid. Instead of using an ear mould, a very thin tube passes the sound into the ear canal, and this is held in position by a small dome.

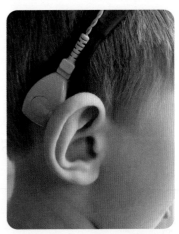

*   **A bone-anchored hearing aid** (BAHA) is used by some children and adults when a conventional hearing aid is not suitable, e.g. for those with no ear canals (atresia). A BAHA can be worn on a headband behind the ear or can be surgically attached to the skull bone behind the ear.

A bone-anchored hearing aid using a soft band

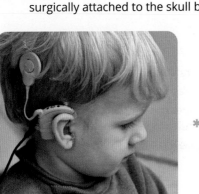

*   **Cochlear implant:** if a child's hearing loss is severe or profound, then surgery may be performed to fit a cochlear implant.

A cochlear implant

DYSLEXIA

A range of specialist aids and equipment is available to children with dyslexia. Computers, tablets and smartphones, and the software they use, can be very useful for children with dyslexia, particularly as they get older. The following is a list of tools which may be useful when working with a child with dyslexia:

* Present typed or written text to children using a simple font such as Arial or Verdana. Always use a font size of at least 12.

* Use cream or another pastel colour for photocopying material for children with dyslexia as text on white paper is much more difficult to read for some children.

Tinted overlays can make reading easier for a child with dyslexia

* Tinted overlays can be used to make reading easier. These can be bought in packs of different colours. Establish which colour works best for the child.

Glasses with tinted lenses can aid a child with dyslexia.

* Some children use glasses with tinted lenses which can make reading easier.

* Reading pens can be useful for children with dyslexia. The pen scans the text, and it reads it to the child.

* Speech recognition software such as Dragon NaturallySpeaking can be used by children, particularly as they get older. The child speaks what they wish to write into a small microphone and their speech is typed. The programme needs to be 'trained' to recognise an individual's voice and accent.

* Spell-check facilities on programmes such as Microsoft Word have a spell-check function, which is extremely useful for children with dyslexia. Make sure it is set to UK English, as the default setting is US English.

* Screen-reading software is widely available. The text is highlighted, and the computer reads it aloud for the child.

Collaborate

In groups, research online some of the products available to assist children with dyslexia. Find out how they benefit the child with dyslexia and how much they cost.

* Picture Exchange Communication Systems (PECS boards) can be used to help children with poor verbal skills to articulate their needs. PECS boards can be homemade so that they are tailored to the needs of the individual child. Commercial PECS boards are also available.

A commerical PECS board

12.4 SPECIALIST AIDS AND EQUIPMENT FOR CHILDREN WITH ADDITIONAL SOCIAL AND EMOTIONAL NEEDS

Generally speaking, for children with additional social and emotional needs, such as ADHD and ASD, the focus is on finding ways to help the child reduce stress and regulate their emotions and behaviour. There is a range of specialist aids and equipment available:

An indoor trampoline

* Indoor play equipment such as trampolines can be used to release energy and reduce stress.

* Therapy balls, spinning tops, fidgets and spinners can all be used to help the child reduce stress and anxiety.

A push-pop fidget toy

* Weighted blankets and pressure vests can be used to give the child a feeling of calm and safety.

A weighted blanket

* Noise-reducing headphones can be used by children who are hypersensitive to sound.

Noise-reducing headphones

* Hideaway areas and sensory 'egg' chairs can be used by children if they are feeling stressed and require some quiet time.

A sensory chair

* It is most beneficial if children with ASD have access to a sensory room. A sensory room is a quiet therapeutic space with a variety of equipment to help children with additional needs such as ASD to feel calm and have a chance to refocus themselves so they can be better prepared for learning and interacting with others. Sensory rooms are often equipped with:

  * Safety wall and floor padding

  * Bubble tubes

  * Fibre-optic lighting

  * Projectors

* Multisensory lighting, e.g. lava lamps
* Sensory ball pools
* Beanbags and sensory cushions
* Soft play products

A well-equipped sensory room

SHOW YOU KNOW

List and explain the purpose of two specialist aids or items of equipment of benefit to children with:

* Additional physical needs
* Additional language and communication needs
* Additional emotional and social needs

Section 4

Qualities, Skills and Strategies

Qualities Required to Work Effectively and Supportively with Children with Additional Needs in the ELC Setting

What I will learn

* The qualities required to work effectively with children with additional needs.

13.1 INTRODUCTION

This chapter highlights the key qualities needed to be an effective special needs assistant (SNA) in an ELC setting. A quality is an innate or an acquired characteristic that determines the nature and behaviour of a person. Working with young children can be both rewarding and challenging. In order to work with children effectively it is important for SNAs to have certain skills and qualities. The most fundamental quality required for working as an SNA is that you love children and enjoy working with them. After this, everything else is easy.

13.2 BE RESPECTFUL

There are many reasons why children with additional needs deserve our respect, but most of all because they are a child, first and foremost. They may act differently, walk differently or think differently to other children but, at heart, they are a child like no other. All children deserve our respect, regardless of ability or disability. Ability or disability is just one difference a person may have, just as a difference such as eye colour or hair colour is only one part of a person. Children with additional needs all have different personalities and capabilities. Look for a child's strengths and you will find them.

13.3 BE NON-JUDGEMENTAL

When working as an SNA, it is important to be non-judgemental and understanding. When difficult situations arise, always try to consider issues from all perspectives. When a child is displaying challenging behaviour, try not to focus on the behaviour but instead look for the cause. Always try and consider situations from the child's perspective.

13.4 BE DISCREET

It is very important when working with children with additional needs to be discreet and respectful of the child. Not all special needs are visible. Young children see only their friends in the ELC setting; they are unaware of any differences. SNAs and ELC professionals need to adopt subtle strategies to ensure no child stands out from the crowd. Where a child with additional needs in a pre-school setting may not be toilet trained, changing the child should be done in an inconspicuous manner.

Collaborate

What qualities do you feel you possess to work with children with additional needs? Think of times when you have used your qualities and discuss them with a partner.

13.5 WORK INCLUSIVELY

The AIM (access and inclusion model) programme is built around the word 'inclusion', and a sense of belonging should be instilled in all children in the ELC setting. When working with children with additional needs, SNAs need to ensure children can take part in as many learning experiences in the ELC setting as feasible. This may mean simplifying tasks or making some minor adjustments but all children need to be given opportunities.

Extend your learning

Research the access and inclusion model on aim.gov.ie and look at the resources they have on inclusive play.

13.6 BE PATIENT

When a child has an additional need, you must have patience. The child may take longer to complete a task or may take longer to show signs of progression in their development, but it is very important for the SNA to be patient as the child will pick up on any signs of an adult becoming impatient with them. This can lead to the child feeling upset, angry, inadequate, frustrated and anxious. Children can pick up on both verbal and non-verbal signals of impatience. Ensure your tone of voice is calm and unhurried, without sounding bored or disinterested. Be careful that your body language is not signalling frustration or impatience. Use positive body language and speak enthusiastically and calmly to the child. When a child says 'I can't', provide encouragement and break the task into steps for the child. Reward a child with positivity, e.g. clapping, saying 'well done', giving the thumbs-up for all progress and effort. Do not insist a child must complete a task if they are clearly struggling.

13.7 HAVE EMPATHY

Empathy is the ability to understand emotionally what another person is feeling, being able to see things from another person's point of view, and imagining yourself in another place or another person's shoes. It is important for an SNA to have empathy, but it is equally important for an SNA to teach children empathy. To do this, they must be role models of empathy in the ELC setting. SNAs need to be able to teach young children about different feelings and emotions. Being able to discuss and describe their feelings will also help children to understand others' feelings.

13.8 BE CONSISTENT/FAIR

When working as an SNA it is very important that, in everything you do and in all your interactions with others, you are consistent and fair. SNAs should be consistent in their interactions with children with additional needs. Good behaviour management policies should ensure that challenging behaviour is dealt with both fairly and consistently. Children learn much better in an environment where the expectations are reachable and clear. You won't always be able to treat children the same but it is very important to treat them all fairly.

13.9 BE CARING AND APPROACHABLE

The best SNA is one with whom the child with additional needs can feel comfortable and develop a bond over time. An SNA needs to be friendly and caring and take an interest in the children's interests. This will all help in ensuring you are more approachable as an SNA. Smile and use a friendly, upbeat tone of voice and manner. Be attentive, listen and observe carefully for what the child is trying to communicate with you.

13.10 BE RELIABLE

An SNA is a vital part of the ELC team and therefore needs to be reliable, dependable and professional at all times. The child, parents and the ELC rely on the SNA to support the child with additional needs. It is vital that an SNA be punctual and dependable. Change of routine can be very upsetting for children with additional needs and although some absences maybe unavoidable, it is in the best interests for everyone in the ELC setting that the SNA is in work for the scheduled days and times.

13.11 VALUE THE CHILD'S INDIVIDUALITY

No two children are the same, regardless of what diagnosis or condition that they may have. Children have different personalities, interests, likes and dislikes and it is up to the ELC professionals working with them to ensure that they are all valued and respected for their uniqueness. Children come from homes that have different beliefs, cultures and customs and we need to ensure that each individual feels valued and respected. The following are important to remember:

* Don't compare children to others.

* Accept that children will like and dislike different things.

* Value the child's talents, preferences and best attributes.

* Accept the child for who they are.

* Support and encourage new interests.

* Give them autonomy, allow them to make choices for themselves.

The Power of Encouraging Words

A group of frogs was travelling through the woods, when two of them fell into a deep pit. All the other frogs gathered around the pit. When they saw how deep it was, they informed the unfortunate frogs that they would never get out. Ignoring their comments, the two frogs started trying to jump out of the pit. The other frogs told them to stop, that they were as good as dead.

Finally, one of the frogs took heed of what the other frogs were saying and simply gave up. He fell down and died. The other frog, however, continued to jump as hard as he could. Once again, the crowd of frogs yelled at him to put an end to his pain and suffering and just accept his fate.

But to the surprise of one and all, he jumped even harder and finally succeeded in getting out of the pit. The other frogs asked him, 'Why did you continue jumping? Didn't you hear us?' To their shock they discovered that the frog was deaf, and all the time he actually thought they were encouraging him to get out. He did not want to disappoint them and therefore did not give up.

This story teaches two lessons:

1. There is the power of life and death in the tongue. An encouraging word to someone who is down can lift them up and help them make it through the day.

2. A destructive word to someone who is down can destroy them. Be careful of what you say.

The power of words is sometimes hard to understand. An encouraging word can go such a long way. Anyone can speak words that tend to rob another of the spirit to continue in difficult times. Special is the individual who will take the time to encourage another. Be special to others. Speak life to those who cross your path.

Read more at: https://www.citehr.com/279-power-words-frog-story.html

SHOW YOU KNOW

1. Why would an SNA need to be non-judgmental?

2. Explain what you understand by the access and inclusion model.

3. Describe why an SNA would need to be patient with a child with an additional need.

4. Explain why it is important to value a child's individuality.

14

Skills Required to Work Effectively and Supportively with Children with Additional Needs in the ELC setting

What I will learn:

* The skills required to work effectively with children with additional needs in the ELC setting.
* Understand the rights of children.
* The steps to be taken when feeding, toileting or dressing a child with additional needs.
* How to promote hygiene in an early years setting.
* The importance of child protection.
* Recognise the importance of continuous professional development.

14.1 INTRODUCTION

The role of an SNA in an ELC environment is a very practical role. This chapter describes the skills that are required to be an effective SNA in an ELC environment. A skill is the ability to do a particular task well and with expertise. It is something that can be learnt.

14.2 OBSERVATION

Observation, whether formal or informal, is a fundamental skill used in any ELC setting to learn about how children are developing and progressing. Observation can be used to understand more about children's behaviour as well as the antecedent or trigger of a child's behaviour. As an SNA, you will need to observe the child/children you are working with very closely every day. In the early days of working with a new child or children, observation will help you get to know the child and learn about their likes and dislikes. One of the most important skills an SNA can have is the ability to observe a child's body language and non-verbal communication, along with their verbal communication, to assess accurately how the child is feeling and whether they understand and are motivated to do what they have been asked to do.

14.3 EXCELLENT INTERPERSONAL SKILLS

To be an effective SNA it is vital that you possess interpersonal skills. Good communication is key: SNAs must be able to communicate with the child, parents, the ELC team and other professionals, e.g. speech and language therapists. There are a number of key skills involved in being a good communicator:

* **Listen actively:** When you are working with any young child it is important that they know you are listening carefully to them. Come down to the child's physical level to have proper eye contact with them. Show that you are interested and listening to them by giving them verbal and non-verbal feedback, e.g. nodding and saying 'OK', 'that's right', etc. Use facial expressions. Active listening also involves remembering what the child is saying and referring to it in future conversations.

* **Be clear and concise:** An effective communicator gets their message across in a clear and concise manner. When communicating with children, use short, clear sentences. You may need to use some aids or props to assist you when communicating with children, e.g. when asking 'Would you like a drink?' point at the child's drink or a picture of a drink. When giving instructions or directions, do not try to communicate too many at once. Too much information at the one time is confusing for some children. Break tasks up into manageable chunks.

* **Be available and pay attention:** Young children need to know that you are available to communicate with them, that you will listen to them and that you will take on board what they are saying to you. However, children also need to be aware that you may not always be able to give them attention when they request it as you might be busy doing a task or speaking with someone else. Children with additional needs need to learn how to be patient and wait their turn too.

* **Be patient:** Some children can have difficulty communicating their needs effectively; other children can have difficulty following instructions and directions. Therefore, it is important for the SNA to be patient. If a child does not appear to be following the instructions, it could be that they do not understand or that they have forgotten what you have asked them to do.

14.4 FIRST AID

A first-aid box

The Child Care Act 1991 (Early Years Services) (Amendment) Regulations 2014 Regulation 25 states that a registered provider must ensure that the service has enough staff appropriately trained in first aid for children and are available in case of any injury or sudden illness. The number of staff with this training will depend on the number and needs of children attending the service and the rosters applied. When working with children with additional needs it is highly recommended for an SNA to have up-to-date first aid training. When working with children with certain conditions, additional training may be necessary, e.g. how to administer medication to a child who has epilepsy. There is also additional first aid training that may be taken, e.g. training on how to use a defibrillator machine. First aid certification must be updated every three years.

14.5 MANUAL HANDLING

Under the Safety, Health and Welfare at Work Regulations 2007, in relation to manual handling training, all employers are required to carry out a risk assessment to determine whether employees require manual handling training. SNAs may face many physical demands, particularly in relation to lifting, when caring for people with additional needs. Children with additional needs sometimes require complex care that demands the application of proper manual handling techniques. These lifting and handling methods must be implemented in ways that ensure the safety of the child and the SNA.

14.6 UNDERSTANDING THE RIGHTS OF CHILDREN

Understanding the rights of the child is the responsibility of all ELC professionals, as Ireland has ratified the UN Convention on the Rights of the Child. It is important that an SNA respect each and every child with whom they work. An SNA must maintain the dignity of every child, be professional and respect confidentiality. As an SNA, confidential information about the child's needs will be discussed with you and it is important to remember the child's right to respect and privacy. The SNA must promote the inclusion of the child in all activities and play in the ELC setting. The SNA needs to ensure the following rights of children are maintained throughout their work:

a. **Survival rights** include the child's right to life and the needs that are most basic to existence, such as nutrition, shelter, an adequate living standard and access to medical services.

b. **Development rights** include the right to education, play, leisure, cultural activities, access to information, and freedom of thought, conscience and religion.

c. **Protection rights** ensure children are safeguarded against all forms of abuse, neglect and exploitation, including special care for refugee children; safeguards for children in the criminal justice system; protection for children in employment; protection and rehabilitation for children who have suffered exploitation or abuse of any kind.

d. **Participation rights** encompass children's freedom to express opinions, to have a say in matters affecting their own lives, to join associations and to assemble peacefully. As their capacities develop, children should have increasing opportunity to participate in the activities of society, in preparation for adulthood.

14.7 FEEDING

Levels of independence regarding feeding vary among children with different special needs. While most children with special feeding needs have physical disabilities, this is not always the case. For example, some children with autism have sensory defensiveness regarding certain tastes and textures and may have special feeding needs.

Before feeding the child:

* Tell the child it is time to eat.

* Wash your hands and the child's face and hands.

* Seat the child in a comfortable position. They should be seated in an upright position, with hips and feet at a 90-degree angle. Try to ensure the child is not slouching, use the seat belt in a high chair and use pillows or towel rolls to support the sides of the child if necessary. The SNA should sit down facing the child at eye level.

* Stay calm, smile at the child and encourage them. Don't show frustrations with any difficulties during the meal. Give lots of praise and reassurance to the child.

Equipment:

* The spoon size should match the size of the child's mouth.

* Use plastic or unbreakable spoons and beakers so that a child with a strong bite reflux does not cause damage.

* Use plates or small bowls that have sections with a lip on the sides to support self-feeders.

* Use sippy cups or mugs with handles for self-feeders, to encourage independence.

* Some children may need a straw.

* Use suction pads for plates and bowls to prevent slipping.

During feeding:

* Check the temperature of the food/drink carefully.

* Tell the child what food you are offering them.

* Follow parental guidance when feeding the child.

* Pureed food should be thick enough not to spill out of the child's mouth.

* Encourage the child to hold the spoon and feed themselves. Remember that a mess can be easily cleaned.

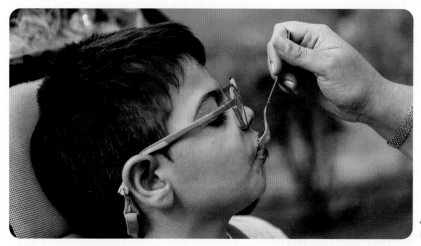

An SNA feeding a child with additional needs

14.8 HYGIENE

Hygiene routines are an important part of work in an ELC setting. SNAs must ensure that the area is safe and clean for both the children and themselves. This helps to prevent infection. Good hygiene routines should be promoted at all times, including as follows:

* **Handwashing:** An SNA should try and teach the child how to wash their hands correctly or assist the child to wash their hands correctly. Using songs is a good way to try to ensure that children wash their hands for an appropriate length of time. Suitable posters, close to sink areas, can encourage children to wash their hands correctly. An SNA too must wash their hands correctly and often, using warm water and soap. If handwashing is not possible, use hand sanitiser.

* SNAs should wash their hands:
    * Before starting work.
    * Before eating, smoking, handling or preparing food or feeding a child.
    * Before preparing food or drink.
    * After using the toilet or assisting a child with toileting.
    * After nappy changing.
    * After playing with or handling items in the playroom.
    * After dealing with bodily fluids, wiping runny noses, cleaning up vomit, etc.
    * After handling waste.
    * After removing disposable gloves or aprons.
* Children should be taught to wash their hands:
    * After using the bathroom.
    * After sneezing, blowing their nose or coughing.
    * After touching an open cut or sore.
    * After playing outside.
    * Before and after eating.

A poster beside the sink can promote good handwashing routines.

* **Hair care:** An SNA with long hair should keep it tied back at all times while in the ECCE setting. Children should also be encouraged to keep their hair back but this can be an issue for a child with autism with sensory issues. In this scenario try to work with the parent/guardian and ensure the child's hair is clean and washed regularly.

* **Nail care and jewellery:** SNAs need to keep their nails short and clean as germs can get trapped underneath longer nails. Nail extensions and false nails are not suitable when working with younger children in an ELC setting. Always use warm water and soap when handwashing and use a nail brush to remove dirt from under fingernails. Use paper towels to dry hands and throw into a closed bin after use to prevent the spread of infection. Jewellery should be kept to a minimum (rings, for example, can trap dirt and germs). It is worth noting that wearing jewellery such as big earrings can also be a potential hazard for an SNA.

* **Cuts and grazes:** Cover any cuts with a waterproof dressing to prevent cross-infection.

* **Equipment:** Ensure all equipment, play materials and areas are cleaned and disinfected regularly.

14.9 DRESSING

When assisting a child with additional needs to dress, it is important to encourage the child to be as independent as possible in putting clothes on and taking them off. Clothes may have to fit under, over or around braces, callipers, harnesses and tubes. Some children with additional needs will have clothing needs:

* **Cerebral Palsy:** a child may need extra padding around the knees or elbows to prevent injury.

* **Epilepsy or brain trauma:** a child may need to wear a helmet to prevent injury from falls or knocks to the head.

* **Eczema:** a child may need protective gloves in cold weather when using art and craft materials.

* **Sickle cell anaemia:** a child will need extra layers in cold weather to lessen the risk of their abnormal blood cells becoming sticky.

* **Down syndrome:** when a child with DS has heart and circulatory issues, they will require extra warm clothing in colder weather.

* **Autism:** a child with autism may have sensory issues with particular types of clothing or tags on their clothes.

14.10 TOILETING

Controlling bladder and bowel movements is always a major achievement on the road to independence. Children with additional needs may be delayed in this area of development. Children will toilet train when they are ready: there is no way to speed up the process. Some children with physical disabilities may require help getting onto and off the toilet, changing incontinence pads or emptying a catheter bag. Children with other additional needs may require help with hygiene but need no physical lifting.

When assisting a child in the toilet:

* Keep the toilet door closed to protect the privacy of the child.

* Before assisting the child with their toilet needs, wash your hands and put on plastic disposable gloves and a plastic apron. Clean down the toilet seat. (Be aware of any allergies to latex, and use latex-free gloves if necessary).

* Ensure your manual handling certificate is up to date. For the health and safety of both the child and the SNA, you must know how to move a child with a physical disability correctly.

* Encourage independence as much as possible. Some wheelchair users can lift themselves to the toilet with handrails. Other children may require the presence of an SNA in case they lose their balance and/or to assist them to clean themselves afterwards or to readjust clothing.

* When moving a child from their wheelchair, position their chair alongside the toilet. The sides of the wheelchair will normally slide down. Moving should be done with the person facing you. Bend your knees and move the child by holding them under your arms. Support the child's weight by holding them against you. Talk to the child and tell them what you are doing. Counting 'one, two, three' can help. Stand beside the child or support them if necessary while they are on the toilet. Do not hurry the child. When they are finished, help the child lean forward so that they can be cleaned. Support them with your body while you are doing this.

* Some children with paralysis from the waist down have little bowel or bladder sensation. They will not know when their bladder is full or when they are having a bowel movement. For this reason, many children wear incontinence pads or nappies every day. SNAs have the responsibility to ensure the child is always clean and fresh during the day.

* Where an incontinence pad is needed, appropriate changing facilities are required. For a young child (0–3 years) in the ELC environment this is done in the nappy-changing area. However, as the child gets older an SNA may have to use a washable changing couch at the same level as the child's wheelchair.

* Used pads or nappies should be disposed of in sanitary bins, for collection by a specialist waste management company.

14.11 CHILD PROTECTION

Child protection is an extremely important topic when working with any children and particularly children with additional needs. The legislation surrounding the Irish Child Protection system is discussed in chapter 9. This section deals with *Children First: National Guidance for the Protection and Welfare of Children,* published by the Department of Children and Youth Affairs (DCYA) in 2017. This guidance is issued under Section 6 of the Children First Act 2015. It is intended that this guidance be implemented side by side with the Children First Act 2015.

The Children First logo

The *Children First: National Guidance for the Protection and Welfare of Children* is underpinned by the Children First Act 2015, and replaces previous editions. Its purpose is to help a general audience recognise child abuse and report a reasonable concern about a child's welfare or protection. It also gives specific information about the statutory responsibilities of individuals who are mandated to report child protection concerns and of organisations that provide relevant services to children.

HOW TO USE THE *GUIDANCE*

The guidance is divided into six chapters. Appendices and references are also included.

* Chapters 1 and 2 are intended for use by all readers. They outline the key messages of the *Guidance* and provide information on recognising and reporting reasonable concerns about the welfare or protection of a child.

* Chapter 3 outlines the legal obligations placed on mandated persons by the Children First Act 2015 and contains guidance about making a mandated report.

* Chapter 4 contains guidance for organisations that provide services to children and young people about their legal requirement under the Children First Act 2015. It outlines how to conduct a risk assessment and prepare a Child Safeguarding Statement. It also contains the details of best practice procedures in child safeguarding that all organisations should consider.

* Chapter 5 describes the roles of Tusla and An Garda Síochána as the statutory bodies with the main responsibility for child welfare and protection. It also outlines what happens after a report of a concern about a child is made to Tusla.

* Chapter 6 identifies the roles and responsibilities of central government and other statutory organisations and structures that monitor the implementation of the Children First Act 2015 and this *Guidance*.

It is advisable for all learners to download the full *Children First: National Guidance for the Protection and Welfare of Children* as only a summary will be provided here. All ELC professionals must complete Tusla's Children First eLearning Programme.

In this *Guidance*, 'a child' means a person under the age of eighteen years, who is not or has not been married.

CHAPTER 1: INTRODUCTION AND USE OF THIS GUIDANCE

The introduction gives the ten key principles that should inform best practice in child protection and welfare:

* The safety and welfare of children is everyone's responsibility.

* The best interests of the child should be paramount.

* The overall aim in all dealings with children and their families is to intervene proportionately to support families to keep children safe from harm.

* Interventions by the state should build on existing strengths and protective factors in the family.

- ∗ Early intervention is key to getting better outcomes. Where it is necessary for the state to intervene to keep children safe, the minimum intervention should be used.

- ∗ Children should only be separated from parents/guardians when alternative means of protecting them have been exhausted.

- ∗ Children have a right to be heard, listened to and taken seriously. Taking account of their age and understanding, they should be consulted and involved in all matters and decisions that may affect their lives.

- ∗ Parents/guardians have a right to respect, and should be consulted and involved in matters that concern their family.

- ∗ A proper balance must be struck between protecting children and respecting the rights of parents/guardians and families. Where there is conflict, the child's welfare must come first.

- ∗ Child protection is a multi-agency, multidisciplinary activity. Agencies and professionals must work together in the interests of children.

(DCYA, *Children First: National Guidance for the Protection and Welfare of Children*, 2017)

CHAPTER 2: CHILD ABUSE – WHAT IS IT? HOW DO I RECOGNISE IT? HOW DO I REPORT IT?

This chapter is intended to be read by everyone who comes into contact with children. Everyone who has dealings with children must be able to recognise the four main types of abuse, and know how to report a concern to Tusla.

'Reasonable Grounds for Concern'

When you work with children you should always inform Tusla when you have reasonable grounds for concern that a child may have been, is being, or is at risk of being abused or neglected. Reasonable grounds for a child protection or welfare concern include:

- ∗ Evidence, for example an injury or behaviour, that is consistent with abuse and is unlikely to have been caused in any other way.

- ∗ Any concern about possible sexual abuse.

- ∗ Consistent signs that a child is suffering from emotional or physical neglect.

- ∗ A child saying or indicating by other means that they have been abused.

- ∗ Admission or indication by an adult or a child of an alleged abuse they committed.

- ∗ An account from a person who saw the child being abused.

(DCYA, *Children First Guidance*, 2017)

Definitions of abuse

This part of the *Guidance* document describes the four main types of child abuse – neglect, emotional abuse, physical abuse and sexual abuse – and offers guidance on how to recognise such abuse. A child could be subjected to one or more forms of abuse at any given time.

Did you know?

Child neglect is the most frequently reported category of abuse, both in Ireland and internationally.

* **Neglect** is defined as an omission of care. It is when a child's health, development or welfare is impaired by the child being deprived of food, clothing, warmth, hygiene, medical care, intellectual stimulation or supervision and safety. Neglect occurs over a period of time rather than one specific event, e.g. a child whose parent forgets to include their water bottle in their school bag one day may be a one-off incident, and this is not considered neglect. However, if a pattern develops where the child's lunch and water is forgotten, then the ELC professional should investigate the issue further. Neglect is associated with poverty but not necessarily caused by it.

* **Emotional abuse** is the systematic emotional or psychological ill treatment of a child as part of the overall relationship between a caregiver and a child. Once-off and occasional difficulties between a parent/carer and a child are not considered emotional abuse. Abuse occurs when a child's basic need for attention, affection, approval, consistency and security are not met, due to incapacity or indifference from their parent or caregiver.

* **Physical abuse** is when someone deliberately hurts a child physically or puts them at risk of being physically hurt. It may occur as a single incident or as a pattern of incidents. Physical abuse can include the following: physical punishment, beating, slapping, hitting or kicking, pushing, shaking or throwing, pinching, biting, choking or hair-pulling, use of excessive force in handling, deliberate poisoning (e.g. with alcohol or medication), suffocation, fabricated/induced illness and female genital mutilation. The Children First Act 2015 includes a provision that abolishes the common law defence of reasonable chastisement in court proceedings. Previously, this defence could be invoked by a parent or other person in authority who physically disciplined a child. The change in legislation now means that, in prosecutions relating to assault or physical cruelty, a person who administers such punishment to a child cannot rely on the defence of reasonable chastisement in the legal proceedings.

* **Sexual abuse** occurs when a child is used by another person for their gratification or arousal, or for that of others. It includes the child being involved in sexual acts (masturbation, fondling, oral or penetrative sex) or exposing the child to sexual activity directly or through pornography. Examples include: any sexual act intentionally performed in the presence of a child, an invitation to sexual touching or intentional touching or molesting of a child's body whether by a person or object for the purpose of sexual arousal or gratification, masturbation in the presence of a child or the involvement of a child in an act of masturbation, sexual intercourse with a child, whether oral, vaginal or anal, sexual exploitation of a child, exposing a child to inappropriate or abusive material through information and communication technology, or consensual sexual activity involving an adult and an underage person.

Concerns which require family support services

Many reports to Tusla will not relate to a child protection risk to the child, but will indicate that the parents/guardians are in need of help because a child's needs are not being met adequately. Tusla has a range of professionals who offer advice and support to families. They include family support workers, social workers, family therapists, social care staff, play therapists and youth workers. These professionals help families work through difficult issues, ensure that children have a stable environment to live in, and provide support for parents who are finding it hard to cope.

Concerns that require child protection intervention

Where serious concerns of ongoing risk of significant harm are identified during the assessment and interventions, or where a social worker has concerns that progress is not being made under the Child Welfare Plan/Family Support Plan, a plan of action is prepared. A Child Protection Conference will be held to decide whether it is necessary to put the child's name on the Child Protection Notification System (CPNS) and if so, to agree a Child Protection Plan.

Child Protection Plan

The Child Protection Plan applies to those children who are listed on the Child Protection Notification System. It is a list of actions that help to reduce the risk of harm to the child and to promote their welfare. The plan makes clear the steps to be taken and identifies who is responsible for each part of the plan. Children on Child Protection Plans continue to live at home, unless it emerges that they are at ongoing risk, or if the Child Protection Plan is deemed not to be working. These cases may result in a decision to remove the child from the home.

CHAPTER 6: OVERSIGHT OF CHILD WELFARE AND PROTECTION

This chapter outlines the roles of central government and government departments in promoting the welfare and safety of children. It describes the structures that are in place across the various government departments to maintain high standards in child welfare and protection. It also details the roles of the key bodies that have an oversight role in relation to the statutory services for children and young people.

14.12 WORK UNDER DIRECTION

It is important for an SNA to be able to work under the direction of others in the ELC team and of parents/guardians. A child with additional needs will have an Individual Education Plan; the SNA must follow the guidance in this plan to support the learning and development of the child. You must be able to take constructive feedback from others.

14.13 RECOGNISE THE IMPORTANCE OF CONTINUOUS PROFESSIONAL DEVELOPMENT

Continuous professional development (CPD) plays an important part of any role or job description: we can all improve! It helps to ensure our knowledge and work practices are kept up to date. There are many ways to implement CPD including attending courses, group meetings, staff meetings and shadowing colleagues or other professionals. Some CPD may be mandatory, e.g. updating first aid and manual handling training. CPD should be an ongoing process throughout your working life. It can also ensure you stay interested in your job as you learn new approaches and gain new ideas and techniques to improve yourself.

SHOW YOU KNOW

1. Explain why an SNA needs to have good observation skills.
2. Discuss how an SNA can show excellent interpersonal skills.
3. How often does a person need to update their first aid training?
4. When did Ireland ratify the United Nations Convention on the Rights of the Child?
5. Describe the step you would take to prepare to feed a child with an additional need.
6. Discuss the importance of good hygiene.
7. Describe the four main types of abuse.
8. What is a 'mandated person'?
9. What are the steps an ELC professional should take when reporting a child protection concern?

Strategies to Support Children with Additional Needs in the ELC Setting

What I will learn

* Strategies to support children with additional needs.
* How to promote partnerships with parents/guardians.
* Liaising with other stakeholders.
* Use of alternative forms of communication.

15.1 INTRODUCTION

This chapter aims to support the SNA in working with children with additional needs in the ELC setting. Each child is unique and has their own individual talents and learning needs. Successful inclusion of the child with additional needs requires understanding appropriate strategies that may support the child's learning and development. It is of vital importance that a partnership between parents/guardians and other stakeholders who may be relevant to understanding the child's needs is developed.

15.2 PARTNERSHIP WITH PARENTS/GUARDIANS

It is important to develop partnership with a child's parents/guardians.

The Síolta user manual states: 'Valuing and involving parents and families requires a proactive partnership approach evidenced by a range of clearly stated, accessible and implemented processes, policies and procedures.' When working with parents it is important to keep the lines of communication open at all times. Parents/guardians hold very valuable information on their child. You need to create a comfortable environment to put the parents/guardians at ease, be a good listener and always take the parents'/guardians' point of view on board. It is important to give regular feedback. Ways of promoting communication include as follows:

* Keep a diary to let parents know about the activities the child took part in, toileting, and food and drink intake. The diary should go home with the child so the parents/guardian can write in any information that may be relevant for the ELC setting.

* Computer applications (apps) allow pictures of the child to be shared safely and with comments. This keeps the parent/guardian in contact with the ELC setting too.

* Regular meetings with parents/guardians, both formal and informal, should be held.

* Artwork can be sent home.

* Information can be passed at drop-off or collection times.

15.3 POLICIES AND PROCEDURES

To comply with the pre-school regulations, every ELC setting is required to have certain policies and procedures. When designing and updating its policies and procedures, an ELC setting needs to ensure that the setting is an inclusive one. All ELC professionals need to implement the policies and procedures.

The inclusion policy and procedures in the early years setting consider the following areas:

ADMISSIONS

* Equal access to all children regardless of their needs.

* Make the service a place where everyone, irrespective of gender, ethnicity, culture, religion, language, sexual orientation, age, ability, disability, family structure and social circumstances, feels welcome and valued.

* The service should be willing to offer and implement the AIM.

CURRICULUM/PROGRAMME

* How will the curriculum meet the needs of children with additional needs?

PLAY MATERIALS/EQUIPMENT

* Is there a need to provide additional play equipment or materials to accommodate additional needs?

* Do the play materials/equipment represent society as a whole, e.g. dolls that represent different levels of ability, ethnicity, etc.

EMPLOYMENT

* Advertising, recruitment selection, interviewing, promotion and access to training all need to be considered in an inclusion policy.

BEHAVIOUR

* The behaviour management policy needs to be inclusive of and fair to all children and needs to ensure the health and safety of all children.

COMMUNICATION WITH PARENTS

* Communication with parents needs to be inclusive and may require more than one method of communication, e.g. an illiterate parent will not be able to read letters or notes sent home; parents whose first language is not English may require information to be translated for them.

ASSESSMENT

* Ensure when assessing children that their additional needs are factored in, e.g. Aistear learning record. Aim to point out the positives about the children.

TRAINING

* Ensure all training needs are identified and provided to staff in a timely manner.

15.4 CHILD EMPOWERMENT

The process of empowerment is to enable the children in your care to achieve their full potential. The access and inclusion model's (AIM) goal 'is to empower pre-school providers to deliver an inclusive pre-school experience to children' (Better Start, 2021). Empowering children to be the best they can be has many rewards for the ELC professional too. Empowerment can boost a child's self-esteem. There are lots of ways you can empower young children but try and ensure you do this within the child's developmental reach.

* Learn all you can about the child, their additional needs, their likes and dislikes, etc.

* Focus on the child's strengths and build on them.

* Give the child choices. For children with communication difficulties, this can be done using pictures, e.g. ask 'would you like to play with sand or blocks?' and encourage them to point to their choice.

* Listen to the child and give them time to tell you their needs and wants.

* Allow the child to take risks within reason, encourage the child to move outside their comfort zone, and challenge them. Be mindful of the child's health and safety but don't wrap them up in cotton wool. Children can learn how to use scissors correctly, pour themselves a drink from a jug, climb up the ladder to the slide, etc.

* Always encourage a child to do their best.

* Allow the child the opportunity to follow their interests, and use these to your advantage, e.g. for a child who needs support developing fine motor skills and who is interested in farm animals, provide art and craft activities based on farm animals, make farm animals out of plasticine, colour pictures of farm animals, etc.

* Encourage perseverance and resilience. Initially make new tasks/activities achievable for the child, then using Vygotsky's idea of the zone of proximal development, build on the child's learning. Encourage the child to persevere to achieve their goals. When things don't go to plan, support the child to learn resilience so that they will try again.

* Work closely with parents/guardians and communicate accomplishments and struggles.

15.5 PREDICTABLE SCHEDULE

Having a predictable schedule or routine for a child with additional needs is very important. The ELC setting should aim to establish a routine for children from the first day. A predictable routine gives reassurance. Children do not have the same concept of time as adults and therefore a predictable routine helps to reassure them. Having a predictable routine does not necessarily mean the same activities have to be done at the same time every day; it can include choices for the children. However, it is good to establish a consistent break/snack time. If the last activity in the day is predictable, the child will know that home time is coming.

A predictable schedule reassures children.

Collaborate

In small groups, put together a suitable routine or schedule for a pre-school setting.

15.6 CHILD OBSERVATIONS

Child observation is a professional skill carried out by ELC professionals to enhance the quality of their practice with young children. Child observations can be done both formally and informally. When working with young children an ELC professional is constantly observing children's behaviour, learning and development, relationships and communication skills. However, it is important that we use formal observations as a tool to support children with additional needs. Recording a child's behaviour and progress can be a very helpful tool. Observation methods include event sample, narrative, time sample, sociogram, checklists and media such as videos. Each observation tool can give you a different picture of a child. If you have concerns about a child's behaviour, for example, an event sample is an appropriate tool. It allows you to record a number of incidents, which may help identify a pattern of behaviour: time of day, day of the week, following certain activities/routines, when a child is tired, who the child is with, etc. This will allow you to intervene to address the challenging behaviour.

NARRATIVE OBSERVATION

A narrative observation is an account of exactly what they child is doing and saying while being observed. It is written in the present tense and involves setting time aside to watch and listen carefully for a designated period of time, which can be anything from five to 30 minutes. It should be as accurate and descriptive as possible. Usually, the observer will write their initial narrative observation roughly and it is advisable to write it up fully as soon afterwards as possible. A narrative observation should avoid perceptions; the observer needs to ensure they write about what the child does and says as accurately as possible. For example:

> TC is sitting on the floor with his legs out in front of him holding a naked Action Man figure in his right hand and Gangrene in his left (earlier TC removed Action Man's space suit). He uses his whole hand to grasp the figures, as they are quite large. He is bashing one off the other as if they are fighting. TC appears to be giving a running commentary on the fight, saying, 'Gangrene, huh ah, Gangrene.' Adult says to TC, 'Ah, don't hit Gangrene.' (Flood, 2021)

TIME SAMPLE

A time sample observation gives a picture of a child's activities, social group and their language interactions at fixed periods. This method of observation enables the observer to take notes at preset regular intervals using preset headings, such as actions (what the child is doing); social group (who the child is with); language (what the child is saying). The target child is observed at fixed time intervals, e.g. every five minutes over a 30-minute period. Time intervals must be predetermined. A time sample can be useful to give an overall snapshot of how a child with additional needs is getting on in an ELC setting. For example:

OBSERVATION			
Time	Action	Social group	Language
15.30	Standing at the side wall of the garden looking towards the other children playing in the garden.	On own	Not speaking
15.35	Walking towards adult A, and then walking back to child A	Adult A, child A	'Teacher, child A [says name of child] has his roll, teacher, child A has his roll.' Adult says, 'Tell child A he shouldn't be eating his roll while running around, he'll choke on it.'

(Flood, 2021)

EVENT SAMPLE

An event sample observation record is usually used to record events involving a particular child whose behaviour is causing concern. This method allows the observer to record the frequency of the unwanted behaviour, whether an incident is provoked/unprovoked, a description of the behaviour and the consequence. An event sample may be carried out over a number of days. It also allows the observer to see who the child is with when the behaviour occurs. After a number of incidents, it may show a pattern as to why the unwanted behaviour is occurring. For example:

OBSERVATION

Date	Time	P/UP*	Antecedent	Description of behaviour	Consequence
13/1	9.22	UP	Child L is sitting alone playing with the shape sorter	TC (Target Child) walks over to child L and pulls the shape sorter off her. Child L stands up and tries to resist. TC pushes her and she falls back to the floor. Child L begins to cry.	Adult A walks over and takes the shape sorter from TC, saying, 'Don't push. You have to wait until Child L is finished, TC.' TC jumps up and down saying, 'No' and then lies face down on the floor, crying.
13/1	10.19	UP	Three children are playing with Duplo	TC sits with the three children. Shortly after joining them, she begins to scatter and throw Duplo.	A goes over and says, 'No, don't throw the bricks TC, you could the hit someone and hurt them. A puts the Duplo back in a pile and takes TC with her by the hand. TC resists, saying, 'No.' A lets go of TC after a few minutes and she returns to the blocks.

* Provoked/unprovoked

(Flood, 2021)

CHECKLIST METHOD

A checklist method uses a range of skills, usually from developmental milestone guides, that are age appropriate to the child being observed. The source of the checklist should always be referenced at the end of the observation. They are useful for observing children's physical and social development where the child's skills and behaviour are easily seen. However, for children with additional needs they should be used with caution because they are based on developmental milestone guides and not all children with additional needs will meet these milestones at the ages suggested for the general population. The observer will usually tick items off the list as they observe the child completing a skill or behaviour. It can also be useful for the observer to briefly record evidence of how they came to the conclusion on whether a child can or cannot do a skill.

For example:

OBSERVATION			
Directions: Put a ✔ beside items you have observed and an x beside those skills that you have observed TC cannot yet master. Put N/O beside items you have not had the opportunity to observe.			
ITEM	OBSERVED?	EVIDENCE	DATE
Prone: can lift head and chest well clear of the floor, supporting with outstretched arms – hands flat on the floor.	✔	TC lifted head well clear of floor when she was placed on the play mat after nappy change	8/10
Prone: can roll over from front to back and (usually) from back to front.	✔	Rolled from front to back when placed on a play mat – did not appear to try to roll back.	8/10
Prone: may pull knees up in an attempt to crawl but will slide backwards.	N/O		

(Flood, 2021)

AUDIO/VISUAL OBSERVATION

Recording a child is a useful way of capturing their language development. It is not suggested for students to use audio observations since the anonymity of the child cannot be preserved. An audio recording can give some very rich material for an observer. An audio or visual observation is a good way of sharing the progress a child with additional needs has made in the ELC setting with the parents/guardians and other professionals. Permission must be sought from parents/guardians before making any recordings of a child. The child should also know they are being recorded.

15.7 LIAISING WITH OTHER STAKEHOLDERS

In the course of working with children with additional needs you may encounter many other stakeholders and professionals. Children with additional needs potentially have many professionals working with them for the child's greater good. As the child will be spending a period of time every day in your care it is important that you know the role of each stakeholder and try to ensure you are taking on board their recommendations. The stakeholders may be part of the multidisciplinary team that work with the child.

GENERAL PRACTITIONER

The general practitioner (GP) has a critical role in the Child Health Screening and Surveillance and Immunisation Programme. The Maternity and Infant Care Scheme provides an agreed programme of care free of charge to all expectant mothers who are ordinarily resident in Ireland. The GP provides an initial examination, if possible before 12 weeks, and a further six examinations during the pregnancy, which are alternated with visits to the maternity unit/hospital. When a baby is born, the GP is responsible for the six-week check-up. Information regarding the delivery, etc. is forwarded from the hospital. The GP is therefore the first point of contact in relation to a child with additional needs. If the GP suspects an additional need, then it is their duty to refer the child on to the appropriate service. Where a parent/guardian has a concern about their child, they may seek the help of their GP at any stage.

PUBLIC HEALTH NURSE

The public health nurse is responsible for child health monitoring, which involves a programme of screening interventions and support for parents, starting at birth and extending through the pre-school years. The public health nurse will receive information about all births through the local maternity hospital, or from a midwife in the case of a home birth. They will arrange an appointment to visit a mother and baby at home within 72 hours of discharge from hospital. In total, there are nine age-related visits offered to children under the Child Health Surveillance Screening Programme. Public health nurses carry out checks to find out if a child is growing properly. They will also check to see if they are able to do things that children of the same age are able to do. The public health nurse will refer any concerns related to the child to the appropriate services for assessment.

SPEECH AND LANGUAGE THERAPIST

A speech and language therapist is specifically concerned with the assessment, diagnosis and management of those who have speech and/or language impairments. Speech and language impairment is one of the most common types of disorder in childhood. Young children who have speech and language difficulties are at risk of continued communication problems as well as associated cognitive behavioural, social and psychiatric difficulties. Children with language impairment are also at high risk for learning difficulties and behavioural problems. This service concerns itself with the prevention and early detection of communication problems. A speech and language therapist will see a child who is presenting with the following difficulties:

* Phonological (speech-sound impairment)
* Developmental language difficulties
* Specific speech and language impairment
* Fluency/stammering
* Autistic spectrum disorder
* Written language disorder
* Cleft palate
* Learning disabilities
* Hearing impairment
* Dysphonia/voice disorder

The speech and language therapist, based on their assessment of a child, will provide recommendations to the parents/guardians and ELC setting on how best to work with the child.

OCCUPATIONAL THERAPIST

Occupational therapists (OT) support a child to join in everyday activities to help them achieve their full potential. They assess a child's fine and gross motor skills in relation to their ability to care for themselves, e.g. feeding, washing and dressing. They can advise on suitable equipment and play materials to help the child be as independent as possible. The OT works with children with a range of additional needs including dyspraxia, developmental coordination disorder, poor fine or gross motor skills, perceptual difficulties, poor concentration and poor movement coordination.

PHYSIOTHERAPIST

The physiotherapist is concerned with the gross motor skills and the mobility of a child. The physiotherapist typically works with children who have cerebral palsy, cystic fibrosis, hydrocephalus, Down syndrome, spina bifida, and children with visual impairment.

PSYCHOLOGY SERVICES

A child with additional needs may come in contact with general psychology services in the community or an educational psychologist. The community psychology service has a focus on prevention, assessment, early detection and intervention for children in difficulty, who may be out of home and who are identified as being at risk or in need of protection. The educational psychologist advises on supports in terms of a child's education for children experiencing learning or behavioural difficulties.

15.8 LEARNING PLANS

An Individual Education Plan (IEP) will normally be compiled to support the learning needs of a child with additional needs. It is compiled in consultation with the parents and any other therapists that are working with the child, e.g. the speech and language therapist. It sets out achievable goals for the child with additional needs in the early years setting. An example of a learning goal is to be able to put on their coat, or to be able to sit for a short period of time working on an activity. The access and inclusion model (AIM) provides a template for ELC providers titled 'My Inclusion Plan'. An IEP includes personal details about the child; space for a list of all stakeholders involved with the child; space to record any meetings or communication about the child; information on the transition to pre-school; space to include the voice of the child; a goal planner; a goal record; a reflection tool on goals; planning for transition to primary school; the voice of the child on the transition to primary school; and consent from the parents/guardians for the sharing of information.

This Goal Planner offers reflective questions that will support the planning and development of goals. Space is available on this page to make notes if needed, which can then be used to inform a goal in the child's Goal Record.

AREA OF DEVELOPMENT

Gross Motor Skills	☐	Expressive Communication	☐
Self Help Skills	☐	Fine Motor Skills	☐
Sensory Experiences	☒	Social Skills	☐
Social And Emotional Wellbeing	☒	Medical Needs	☐
Receptive Communication	☐		

Reflect on the child's participation and note areas or skills you feel require support.

Lily runs around the preschool room frequently and leaves group activities to run and jump.

What current strategies or resources support the child in relation to this goal?

We encourage the sensory box and tuff tray where sand, rice and putty are available.

Encouraging Lily to run when in the outdoor environment.

PARTICIPATION

ACCESS

SUPPORT

Consider other key people who could offer essential information to guide you and the child in this process.

Key person to contact:
Occupational Therapist and link with Lily's parents.

Reflect on the 'Voice of the Child' page to identify strengths and interests that will support the child with this goal. Remember, these will change over time.

Strengths: Gross motor skills and fine motor skills.

Interests: Running outside, playdough and water play.

How are we going to achieve this goal?
Identify times when Lily requires support to increase engagement and participation.

Increase movement breaks throughout the day.

Include group movement games.

How do these strategies and resources help the child?

Lily appears more focused and can participate for longer after engaging in these experiences.

The AIM/Better Start goal planner

15.9 CURRICULUM PLANNING

Curriculum 'refers to all learning experiences, whether formal or informal, planned or unplanned, which contribute to a child's development' (National Council for Curriculum and Assessment [NCCA], 2004:2). Depending on the condition or diagnosis of the child with additional needs you may need to use different strategies to support their learning and development. The needs and goals outlined in the child's Individual Education Plan (see 15.8 above) must be built into your curriculum planning. Aistear is the national curriculum framework for children from birth to six years. It 'provides information for adults to help them plan for and provide enjoyable and challenging learning experiences, so that all children can grow and develop as competent and confident learners within loving relationships with others. Aistear describes the types of learning (dispositions, values and attitudes, skills, knowledge, and understanding) that are important for children in their early years, and offers ideas and suggestions as to how this learning might be nurtured.' (Aistear, 2009 p.6)

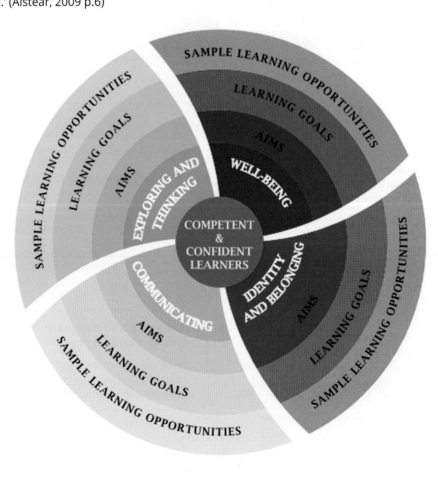

15.10 MANAGING TRANSITIONS

Transition times are when a child has to move from one activity or place to another, e.g. when a child is waiting to go to break time after completing jigsaws. Transitions are often viewed as a time between activities, rather than an activity itself. Transition times can be difficult for young children to manage. They can be unsure what is going to happen next and may feel threatened by the increased noise and activity level. This can make it harder for the child to refocus when a new activity begins.

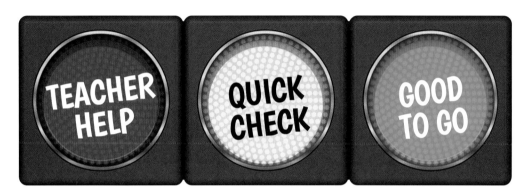

Using a traffic-light system can help with transition time.

Strategies for managing transitions include:

1. Using a clear signal to mark the end of one activity and the beginning of another, such as a sound like a bell, a song, a gesture or an object like a puppet that is used only during this time. Depending on the needs of the children in the ELC setting you may need to use more than one signal, e.g. a child with a hearing impairment might not hear a song being sung.

2. Only using one direction at a time, e.g. instead of saying, 'Get your apron. Then go and take a place at the painting table', say, 'Get your apron', then wait until the task is completed before saying, 'Now go and take a place at the painting table.'

3. Supporting the child with positive affirmations as they move from one activity to another to let them know they are doing well.

4. A visual timetable may help some children cope during transition times. The timetable should contain pictures/photographs of the activities for that day. This helps the child to understand what is coming next.

5. Using a traffic-light system may help the children understand how much time they have left at an activity, e.g. green indicates the activity is open to play, orange indicates that it will be finishing soon, and red indicates clean-up time.

6. For children who struggle with transitioning into circle time/group activities, putting their picture on their chair can give a sense of security by letting them know that their chair is waiting for them.

15.11 INCLUSIVE PLAY, AND APPROACHES PROVIDING EQUALITY OF OPPORTUNITY

Young children learn about their world through play; it is what they do best. Play helps young children in all areas of their development, including physical, cognitive, creative, language, social and emotional growth. Play opportunities in the ELC setting should always be adaptable to the children's needs, to ensure that they all have positive learning experiences. Some children with additional needs require support during play activities for the following reasons:

* They may be unfamiliar with the play materials and may be unsure what to do with them.

* They may be overwhelmed with the number of choices and may have difficulty selecting a toy.

* They may have limited concentration and poor task persistence.

* Increased noise levels during playtime may be stressful for some children.

* The materials may not be developmentally appropriate and therefore the child may not engage with them. This limits their play experiences and opportunities to engage with peers.

* They may be unwilling to engage in trial-and-error exploration.

* They may feel threatened by the close proximity of their peers.

(Klein *et al.*, 2001, p. 136)

Some strategies that may be useful to ensure an inclusive play environment include:

* **Using assistive technology:** Assistive technology can make play and the play environment more accessible for the child with additional needs. Examples of assistive technology are: tablet devices, digital books, computerised augmentative alternative communication systems and Picture Exchange Communication System (see section 15.14 for more information).

* **Trial-and-error exploration:** Some children with additional needs may need encouragement to engage in trial-and-error exploration of toys and they may have low levels of task persistence. Playing alongside a child and following their lead allows the ELC professional to guide the child into the play activity and develop persistence.

* **Teaching a child how to play with toys:** Some children may not know how to play with certain toys, which limits their opportunities for learning and interacting with other children. Sitting with the child and demonstrating how to play with a toy will give the child the skills and confidence to try and play with the toy on their own in the future.

* **Building language skills:** Specific strategies to support vocabulary, concepts and sentence structure can be incorporated into play activities. Using key words and phrases that clearly describe what the child is doing, repeating those words and expanding on the language the child uses are all important in developing language.

* **Encouraging peer interactions:** Some children with additional needs can be reluctant to engage in play with their peers and may need support and encouragement to do so. Free play can be particularly stressful for a child with additional needs. They may feel overwhelmed and threatened by close proximity of other children. An ELC professional may help by creating a personal space for the child, whereby the child can sit on a favourite blanket or mat, and other children learn to not cross the boundary of the blanket unless the child asks them to.

* **Ensure the room is well organised, predictable and clearly marked:** A well-organised room will have space for a child with a physical disability to move around. It is also beneficial for a child with autism as the environment is predictable and play items can be easily found.

* **Pace the activities:** You may need to pace or slow down demonstrations, explanations, tasks and activities to include the child with additional needs. Consider the rate at which you speak and move. Allow extra time for the child to respond or complete a task.

* **Scaffolding:** Scaffolding means supporting a child to succeed at a task they cannot yet complete on their own. The ELC professional should follow the child's lead, supporting and demonstrating as necessary when the child does not know what to do next.

* **Task analysis:** This is the technique of breaking tasks into small steps and then assisting the child to learn one step at a time.

* **Practice and repetition:** Practice and repetition are two of the most effective learning tools for a child with additional needs. All learning involves trial and error, and through practice and effort a child will master a task.

* **Always listen attentively and with interest:** Always listen attentively to a child, even one whose sounds are difficult to understand. You want to encourage the child to practise their language. Showing interest in the child and what they are saying will help build the child's confidence.

15.12 POSITIVE REINFORCEMENTS

The use of positive reinforcement is an unbelievably valuable strategy in working with all children. Everybody likes to be praised and acknowledged for trying their best. The way we do this sends an important message to children. Their learning is significantly influenced by their self-confidence and self-esteem. Using positive language, rewarding children with praise, stickers, stamps, prizes, star charts, etc. are all effective ways of praising and rewarding children's efforts, behaviour and completed tasks.

15.13 POSITIVE BODY AND VOICE TONE

Positive body language and voice tone make you appear friendlier and more inviting to young children.

* Smile. Some of us don't smile naturally, so work on developing this habit.

* Avoid crossing your arms, stuffing your hands in your pockets, or other body positions that make you appear closed off and unapproachable.

* Stand up (or sit up) straight. This makes you look friendlier and also gives your voice a more pleasant, confident tone.

Speaking to children in a warm, pleasant tone will make you much more relatable and the children will embrace it.

The power of positive body language

15.14 ALTERNATIVE AND AUGMENTATIVE METHODS OF COMMUNICATION

Communication is a two-way process. Children with additional needs have to be able to communicate with the adult and the adult needs to be able to communicate with them. For some children the process of communicating can be challenging. It is important for the ELC setting to find ways of communicating with the children they are working with. Alternative and augmentative methods of communication refer to systems and devices that aid communication for people who find it difficult to speak. General rules for communicating with children with additional needs are as follows:

* If you are asking a child a question, ask the child, not their carer.

* Kneel so that you are at the same level as the child when communicating with them.

* Do not cover your mouth when talking and avoid having light coming from behind you, as this casts your face in shadow so facial clues will be more difficult for the child to read.

* Speak clearly, but not in a very loud or exaggerated way.

* Give the child time to respond.

* Do not use an overly sophisticated general vocabulary.

* Learn and use alternative means of communication if the child cannot communicate through speech, e.g. Irish Sign Language, Lámh or PECS.

There are several strategies that can be used to support communication with a child with additional needs including as follows:

COMPUTERISED AUGMENTATIVE ALTERNATIVE COMMUNICATION SYSTEMS

Sometimes called synthetic speech devices, these allow the child to either spell out what it is they wish to communicate or pick from a range of pictorial or symbolic messages on a display. If the child can use their hands, they will press the keys manually. If the user is unable to do this, then on some systems a red light moves along from one picture or symbol to the next on display, and when the correct picture or symbol is arrived at, the child presses down on a large pressure-sensitive button. The device then speaks what the user has indicated.

Technology can help a child with additional needs to communicate.

PICTURE EXCHANGE COMMUNICATION SYSTEM (PECS)

A picture exchange communication system is a form of augmentative and alternative communication. Children using PECS are taught to approach another person and give them a picture of a desired item in exchange for that item. By doing so, the child is able to initiate communication. This enhances their communication abilities and understanding of the function of communication.

A picture exchange communication system (PECS)

THE TREATMENT AND EDUCATION OF AUTISTIC AND COMMUNICATION HANDICAPPED CHILDREN (TEACCH)

TEACCH is a system of structured teaching that was first developed in 1972 by Dr Eric Schopler and his team at the University of North Carolina, USA. The main aim of the TEACCH programme is to help people with autism to live or work more effectively at home, at school and in the community. The method called 'Structured TEACCHing' is based on the unique learning needs of people with ASD, including:

* Strengths in visual information processing.

* Difficulties with social communication, attention and executive function.

RADIO HEARING AIDS

Radio hearing aids can be useful for children with mild hearing loss as they can be used in conjunction with the child's hearing aid. They can make it easier for the child to concentrate on the sounds or voices that you want them to hear. The ELC professional will wear a transmitter that is tuned into the child's hearing aid.

LÁMH

Lámh is a manual sign system designed for children with intellectual disabilities in Ireland. Lámh signs are a simplified version of Irish sign language and are used to support speech. In order to provide an inclusive learning environment the ELC professional could teach all the children songs that include Lámh.

IRISH SIGN LANGUAGE

Irish sign langauge (ISL) has been used by the Irish deaf community for at least 150 years in Ireland and Northern Ireland. ISL is like any other language, such as English or Spanish, in that it has all the features of language, e.g. grammar (rules about word endings, plurals, etc.) and syntax (rules about word order in sentences). Like all languages, ISL has its own alphabet. The alphabet can be used to spell out words but also forms the basis of many of its 4,000 signs.

> ### Did you know?
> - Irish sign language is different from all other sign languages such as British sign language, American sign language, etc.
> - Irish sign language is the first and/or preferred language of 5,000 deaf people in Ireland and approximately 40,000 people in general communicate in ISL (family, friends, co-workers, etc).
>
> (www.irishdeafsociety.ie)

15.15 VISUAL AIDS

Visual aids refer to using a picture, chart or other visual item to communicate with a child who has difficulty understanding or using language. Visual supports can be photographs, drawings, objects, written words or lists. Visual aids can help children who have difficulties interacting with others, using language, and children with repetitive behaviours or limited interests. Story boards can be used to support communication. Ensure you have pictures for all activities/interests/events that happen in the ELC setting and allow the child to choose what activity they want to do. Alternatively, you can use the story board to let the child know what is happening next.

Collaborate

In groups of two or three, design a visual chart that could be used in an ELC setting to help a child understand the routine.

173

15.16 TEACHING SOCIAL SKILLS/SOCIAL STORIES/CIRCLE TIME

SOCIAL SKILLS

Children with additional needs often need to be taught the social skills for coping in different situations. Social skills are important to help the child succeed in all aspects of their lives. According to the National Council for Special Education (NCSE), the following are skills we should teach children with additional needs:

* Taking turns.
* Using eye contact.
* Understanding and using facial expressions.
* Using people's names.
* Helping others.
* Celebrating winning and accepting losing games.
* Sharing.
* Asking for help.
* Using appropriate tone and volume of voice.
* Resolving conflicts.
* Active listening.
* Staying on topic.
* Sharing ideas.
* Waiting patiently.

In order to teach children these skills the NCSE recommend to:

1. Work on one skill at a time.
2. Teach the skill.
3. Practise the skill.
4. Give the student feedback.

SOCIAL STORIES

A social story is a short story written in a specific style and format. It typically describes what happens in a specific social situation. This may be something that is obvious to us but not to a child with impaired social understanding. Social stories aim to improve the child's understanding of social situations and encourage appropriate responses. Social stories can include a combination of writing, pictures and/or symbols to facilitate the communication levels of the child they are intended for, i.e. level of understanding, vocabulary knowledge, etc.

Extend your learning

Carol Gray has written extensively about the benefits of social stories. You can get further information about her work at https://carolgraysocialstories.com.

CIRCLE TIME

Circle time is a short period when children gather as a group in the ELC setting with the ELC professional to listen to and talk with one another. It provides opportunities for children to develop a wide range of skills including social, communication and thinking skills. There are many benefits to circle time including:

* Helping children learn the names of others in the group.
* Helping children with limited attention span and concentration when participating in group activities.
* Promoting a positive sense of self and others.
* Providing structure, predictability and routine for all the children in the setting.

Suggestions for making the most out of circle time include as follows:

* Speak slowly and clearly at all times.
* Use props, pictures and different tones of voice to appeal to all the children.
* Circle time activities should involve a mixture of listening and activity on the part of the children.
* Give time for the children to respond to questions.
* Plan seating carefully.

Circle time in an ELC setting

175

15.17 BEING AWARE OF ENVIRONMENTAL TRIGGERS

Being aware of environmental triggers through the use of observation can allow an SNA to reduce the impact of these triggers on the child with additional needs. Children can have sensory issues – to noise, to certain light, to food, textures, etc. Knowing and understanding these triggers can help an SNA to support a child when they are upset as a result of an environmental trigger. For example, in an ELC environment, children sometimes cry, scream and get upset but this noise may trigger a reaction in a child with additional needs. An SNA needs to understand and learn from parents/guardians about what environmental triggers the child may have. They may have to observe a child to identify environmental triggers. The SNA must help the child learn how to cope with environmental triggers, e.g. using breathing techniques or giving the child an object they find comforting. Avoiding environmental triggers may be a short-term solution; teaching the child coping mechanisms is much more beneficial in the long term.

SHOW YOU KNOW

1. List the policies in which a setting will need to show inclusive practice.

2. In what ways can an ELC practitioner help a child to reach their full potential?

3. Explain the importance of child observation when working with a child with an additional need.

4. Name and describe one observation method.

5. What does a speech and language therapist do to support children with additional needs?

6. What is an Individual Education Plan (IEP)?

7. Why would a child need an IEP in an early years setting?

8. Explain two strategies for managing transitions.

9. What is meant by the term 'scaffolding'?

10. Explain your understanding of PECS.

11. Why is it important to be aware of environmental triggers for a child with additional needs?

Section 5

Importance of Relationships and Teamwork

Building Relationships to Support Children with Additional Needs

16.1 INTRODUCTION

'Parents are the primary educators of the child and have a pre-eminent role in promoting her/his wellbeing, learning and development' (Centre for Early Childhood Development & Education (CECDE), 2006 p. 6). It is important that the ELC setting values the role of parents. Open, honest and respectful partnership with parents is essential in promoting the best interests of the child. Relationships that are based on trust and respect enable parents and caregivers to share information and insights, as well as plan together for the child's future learning and development (National Council for Curriculum and Assessment (NCCA), 2004).

16.2 THE ROLE OF PARENT/GUARDIAN AS THE CHILD'S PRIMARY CAREGIVER AND EDUCATOR

Parents know more about their child and their child's needs than anyone, so it is important to listen to and value what parents have to say. The parent/guardian plays an important role in advocating for the child with additional needs in all aspects of the child's life. It is important for ELC professionals to remember that parents:

* Are the first and primary educators and carers of their child.

* Know and understand their own child best.

* Have specific legal responsibilities towards their child.

* Give their child a strong sense of identity and belonging.

(Meggitt *et al.*, 2016 p. 42)

Section 6 of the Guardianship of Infants Act, 1964 sets out legal responsibilities regarding children born to married parents by stating that the father and mother of an infant are guardians of the infant jointly.

If a child is born outside marriage, the mother is the automatic guardian. The position of the unmarried father of the child is not as certain. An unmarried father will automatically be a guardian if he has lived with the child's mother for 12 consecutive months after 18 January 2016, including at least three months with the mother and child following the child's birth.

16.3 WORKING IN PARTNERSHIP WITH PARENTS

The ELC setting should always work in partnership with all parents. ELC staff act *in loco parentis* when caring for children in the setting. It is, therefore, very important that ELC staff develop and build positive relationships with the parents of children with additional needs. A fundamental part of this partnership is the sharing of knowledge, both practical and strategic, between the parents and the ELC staff regarding the child with additional needs. Parents for their part provide an ELC setting with lots of valuable information about the child, for example:

* Strategies that work with their child.

* Useful equipment.

* Resources they use at home to support their child's learning and development.

* Information on the child's strengths, needs, likes, dislikes, habits and other relevant information.

* Information about the child's family, e.g. siblings, grandparents, pets, etc.

Working in partnership with parents benefits everyone.

The type of general information the ELC setting should be sharing with the parents of a child with additional needs includes:

* How the 'key person' approach works.

* Outline and explanation of approaches to teaching and learning.

* How information will be shared between parents and the ELC setting.

* Monthly curriculum plans.

* Policies and procedures.

* The types of equipment, materials and activities that are offered.

* Observations, or any formal or informal assessment carried out on the child.

'The key person approach in early years is a method of care in which each child is assigned a particular educator who will act as their "go to" person. This person will support the child and their family when they are first integrating into the setting and will continue to be the key person for routine care and for moments of emotional intimacy, building up a secure attachment with the child.'

(Barnardos, 2016 p. 2)

16.4 BUILDING A PARTNERSHIP WITH PARENTS/GUARDIANS

Getting to know a family is especially important in developing a partnership with parents/ guardians. It will help the ELC professional to understand the child too. It is essential both for parents/guardians and the ELC setting to recognise the unique role they each play in the child's life. ELC professionals have knowledge of general child development, and the parents/guardians know their own child best. The parents and family are particularly important to the child and there will be an emotional bond between them. ELC professionals need to develop a warm and affectionate relationship with the child but they should not seek to replace a parent.

Developing mutual trust is the key to forming a true partnership with the parents. It is important to remember, though, that you want to build a *professional* relationship with the parents: although you will be friendly, you are not trying to make friends with parents/guardians. You will need to get to know parents and the family to be able to support a child with additional needs. Information that you might need to know could include:

* Information on important people in the child's life, i.e. siblings, grandparents, friends, pets.
* General interests and activities that family take part in, e.g. every Sunday they go swimming.
* Religion/culture.
* Occupations of parents/guardians.

This information will help you to get to know and understand a child you are working with, but should only be used in that context.

Building a partnership with parents/ guardians in the ELC setting

16.5 SHARING INFORMATION WITH PARENTS/GUARDIANS

Developing effective communication systems between parents/guardians and ELC professionals is important from day one. Information sharing is a two-way process and will be both formal and informal. Information sharing will happen at the beginning of a partnership, at regular set times during the year and on an ongoing daily basis. There are many ways information can be shared between the ELC setting and the parents including as follows:

* **Diary or journal:** A simple but effective strategy is to send a simple notebook home with the child each day into which the ELC practitioner and parents can write comments. It allows for two-way communication to both give and receive information about the child. It may also serve to generate strategies that meet new challenges as they arise.

* **Noticeboard:** Have a noticeboard at the entrance to the setting that displays information about new activities and new topics. This can help parents/guardians prepare the child for what is coming next. It may also allow parents to practise a new song, for example.

* **News time/circle time:** Many settings will include a news time for children each morning, where children are invited to share news with the group. Some children with additional needs may find this difficult or challenging and may be excluded from this activity due to language/communication/memory difficulties. Parents/guardians could facilitate the successful inclusion of the child in this activity by providing the child with a picture or photo that can be used as a memory prompt. The parent could also tell the practitioner about something that happened to the child, and the practitioner could share the news with the group.

* **Open-door policy:** Welcoming parents/guardians into the setting to help out can be a confidence booster for a child but it can also be a rewarding and informative experience for the parent/guardian. Some ELC settings have a daily/weekly rota for parents who are willing and free to help out. Parents can share talents such as music, dancing and occupations with the group. Parents could also be invited to accompany the ELC setting on trips outside the setting.

* **Newsletter:** A monthly newsletter could be sent home informing parents about what the children have been up to in the previous month, and giving the parents an insight into the plan for the coming month.

* **Mobile device apps:** Technology has advanced and apps such as TeachKloud can be used to share information with parents including pictures, accident/incident reports and policies, etc.

A noticeboard at the entrance to the ELC setting is one way of sharing information with parents/guardians.

REFLECTIVE PRACTICE

Thinking about a child with additional needs, reflect on the benefits to parents when an ELC setting shares information about their child.

16.6 BENEFITS OF PARTNERSHIP FOR CHILDREN

When the ELC setting and the parents/guardians have a good relationship and rapport with each other, there are many benefits for the child with additional needs. A partnership helps ELC practitioners to tailor their service around the specific needs of the child in their care. Strategies for learning can be shared between the practitioners and the parents/guardians to ensure consistency, which can be very beneficial for children with additional needs because it will mean learning can be continued at home. The expectations for the child with additional needs will be consistent in both their home and early years environments, e.g. in relation to behaviour. When children know there is a good partnership, it helps them to feel secure and comfortable in the ELC setting. Ultimately, good partnerships benefit the child in helping them reach their full potential.

When the parents/guardians and ELC setting have a good rapport, it builds the child's trust.

16.7 BENEFITS OF PARTNERSHIP FOR THE FAMILY

Like the benefits of partnership with parents, when an ELC setting involves the family it can make the settling-in period much easier for the child, e.g. displaying photos in the setting of the child's family can be reassuring to children. Photos of children's families could include pictures of parents, siblings, grandparents, other extended family or pets. Photos can also provide opportunities to promote language and communication for the child with additional needs. Family members can offer new and interesting learning experiences for the child in an ELC setting, e.g. a family member could be a member of the fire service and could organise a visit to a local fire station, or a family member could be a musician and play music for the children in the ELC setting. Families can play a significant role in children's lives, particularly siblings, and stories about what the child and siblings get up to often come up during news time. It is, therefore, important that the ELC practitioner is aware of family members who play a significant role in children's lives. If siblings are with parents during drop-offs or collections, it is important for the ELC practitioner to be able to greet the siblings too.

16.8 BENEFITS OF PARTNERSHIP FOR THE ELC PRACTITIONER

The ELC practitioner can benefit hugely from having a positive partnership with parents/guardians and families of a child with additional needs. It ensures the ELC practitioner is:

* Well informed about the child with an additional need.
* Able to plan to meet the needs of the child with additional needs.
* Supported in curriculum planning.
* Enabled to maintain consistency between the ELC setting and the home environment.

Extend your learning

The NCCA provides information for parents on ways to extend children's learning on its website (https://ncca.ie/en/early-childhood/for-parents/). This is available in a number of languages.

16.9 THE MULTIDISCIPLINARY TEAM

The multidisciplinary team plays an important role in the life of a child with an additional need. Members of a multidisciplinary team are professionals from a range of disciplines that provide specific services to a child. They will work independently with a child and will come together to provide an individual education plan or care plan for a child with additional needs. Members of the multidisciplinary team could include the general practitioner (GP); public health nurse; speech and language therapist; occupational therapist; physiotherapist; psychology services; social worker; early years practitioner; and the child's parent/guardian.

The multidisciplinary team will come together to put a plan in place for the child with additional needs and will work with each other to come up with appropriate strategies and actions to help the child with additional needs to achieve their full potential. The members of the multidisciplinary team will vary depending on what professionals the child is working with, e.g. a young child with autism is likely to be working with a child psychiatrist, speech and language therapist, occupational therapist, psychologist, social worker, public health nurse and GP. They are diverse professional groups who work together in order to collaborate, reflect, access and support children's learning, development and health. The needs of the family are also considered by the multidisciplinary team.

A multidisciplinary team preparing an Individual Education Plan for a child with additional needs

Having the multidisciplinary team come together is hugely beneficial to the early years service and the child with additional needs as it enables the ELC practitioners to ensure the child's needs are met through the curriculum that they offer.

SHOW YOU KNOW

1. Who are the child's primary educators?
2. Describe what information a parent should provide an ELC setting with before a child enters an ELC setting.
3. Explain your understanding of the Key Person Approach.
4. Discuss four ways information can be shared between the ELC setting and parents.
5. How do good partnerships benefit children?
6. What are the benefits of partnerships with parents for the ELC practitioner?
7. Describe the roles of the multidiciplinary team.

Impact of Additional Needs on the Family

17.1 INTRODUCTION

From the moment a child's family receive a diagnosis of an additional need for their child, it can stir up a vast range of emotions. Some children will receive a diagnosis before birth or when the child is born, e.g. a child with Down syndrome, whereas for other children it can take some time to get a diagnosis, e.g. autism. Either way, it opens a new world for the child's parents. In some cases, it can initially cause a significant amount of physical and psychological stress for parents/guardians and the family. There is a fear of the unknown and the worry of what this diagnosis will mean. Each additional need and diagnosis is different and can cause varying stressors on the family. Parents will need support from health professionals, other family members and support groups or other parents who have a child with the same additional need, and all of these can be invaluable. For some parents, when the child receives a diagnosis, it can be a relief, e.g. for a child with ADHD (Attention Deficit Hyperactivity Disorder) or autism, while others may find it difficult. It is best to give parents time to come to terms with the news that their child has an additional need.

17.2 FINANCIAL IMPACT OF ADDITIONAL NEEDS ON THE FAMILY

When a child is diagnosed with additional needs, life must still go on and parents will still have financial commitments to meet. The financial impact for parents with a child with additional needs will vary, depending on the level of care the child will require. For some parents, it could mean one parent having to take a career break from work or to resign from their position, as the child may have a range of issues that must be addressed. Varying levels of healthcare appointments could make it impossible for either parent to continue to work. This can lead to additional stresses on the family finances and could result in a drastic change in the standard of living the family is used to. For some children with additional needs, waiting lists for specialists can be long and some parents will choose to access private services, which again can be costly.

17.3 ALLOWANCES AND ENTITLEMENTS

Parents may be entitled to some supports and allowances from the Department of Social Protection, the HSE and Revenue Commissioners to help care for their child with additional needs.

DOMICILIARY CARE ALLOWANCE

Domiciliary Care Allowance is a monthly payment to the carer of a child with a disability so severe that the child requires care and attention and/or supervision substantially in excess of another child of the same age. This care and attention must be provided so that the child's activities of daily living are met. The requirement of this level of care and attention must be for at least 12 months.

> **Did you know?**
>
> The current rate of Domicillary Care Allowance is €309.50 per month. From January 2022 the Domiciliary Care Allowance will be €314.50 per month.

CARER'S ALLOWANCE

Carer's Allowance is a payment to people living in Ireland who are looking after someone in need of support because of their age, physical or learning disability or illness, including mental illness. The Carer's Allowance is not payable to everyone: it is mainly aimed at carers on low incomes who live with and look after certain people in need of full-time care and attention. Those on Carer's Allowance may also be entitled to household benefits such as a fuel allowance, free television licence, free telephone rental allowance and a free travel pass.

RESPITE CARE GRANT

The Respite Care Grant is an annual cash payment made by the Department of Social Protection to certain carers for use as they wish.

CARER'S BENEFIT

Carer's Benefit is a payment made to insured persons (those who have been paying PRSI) in Ireland who leave the workforce to care for a person(s) in need of full-time care and attention. Carer's Benefit is payable for a total period of 104 weeks for each person being cared for and can be taken in one or more blocks.

HOMEMAKER'S SCHEME

The Homemaker's Scheme makes it easier for a homemaker to qualify for the state pension (contributory). A homemaker is a person who gives up work to care for a child (under 12) or someone who has a disability.

MEDICAL CARD

A medical card may be issued by the HSE to the parents of children with additional needs or to the child themselves if they are over 16. A medical card allows the holder to receive certain health services free of charge:

* Free GP (family doctor) services

* Prescribed drugs and medicines (with some exceptions)

* Inpatient public hospital services; outpatient services and medical appliances

* Dental, optical and aural services

* Maternity and infant care services

* Some personal and social care services, e.g. public health nursing, social work services and other community care services

INCAPACITATED CHILD TAX CREDIT

Tax credits can be claimed by a parent or guardian in respect of a child who is permanently incapacitated, either physically or mentally, from maintaining him- or herself.

REVENUE ALLOWANCES AND VAT REFUNDS

Various tax and VAT refunds are available to the parents of children with additional needs, e.g. if necessary modifications are made to the house to accommodate the child or if a specific vehicle has to be purchased to accommodate a wheelchair.

Check out www.revenue.ie for all up-to-date rates and allowances.

17.3 EMOTIONAL/SOCIAL IMPACT ON THE FAMILY

Having a child with an additional need can affect the whole family in different ways. On the one hand, it can broaden horizons, increase family members' awareness of their inner strength, enhance family cohesion and encourage connections to community. On the other hand, the time and emotional demands of caring for a child with additional needs can take a toll on families. Parents who are full-time carers of a child with additional needs may suffer from sleep deprivation; they may have very little free time for themselves or time to spend with other children in the family; they may lose a sense of their own identity as they may not have time to pursue their own personal interests or hobbies, or to spend time with their partner or friends. Caring for a child with additional needs can put huge strains on a couple's relationship, and can cause feelings of guilt for not giving other children in a family enough time. The impacts will depend on the child's condition and its severity, as well as the physical, emotional and financial means of the family and the resources that are available to them.

For families, the stress involved in caring for a child with additional needs may take its toll on mental and physical health. There can be feelings of guilt, blame or reduced self-esteem for all members of a family. A change to the standard of living as a result of costs associated with medical care and other services can have emotional and social repercussions for all members of the family. Siblings may feel left out and their lives may also be adversely affected. Parents may not have the time or money to keep them involved in their extracurricular activities.

On the positive side, families may join support groups and meet a whole new circle of friends. This can be a great support for all members of a family. For example, Down Syndrome Ireland have many branches all over the country where parents and families meet and have regular outings with each other. A child with additional needs can open up lots of new doors and opportunities for their families that they may never have dreamt about before.

17.4 PHYSICAL IMPACT ON THE FAMILY

As a child with a physical additional need gets older, the demands on their family will grow as they try to meet the basic needs of the child. There can be challenges in lifting a child for daily living activities; families may need a car that can accommodate a wheelchair; the physical layout of a house may no longer be suitable to meet the child's needs, e.g. they may need a bedroom at ground-floor level or bathrooms may need to be altered; families may need to move house in order for the child's needs to be sufficiently met, which can be upsetting for other family members if they are uprooted from their friends and extended family members. The child's needs will change as they get older and heavier, which can lead to the risk of injury for family members who assist in the physical care of the child, e.g. back problems.

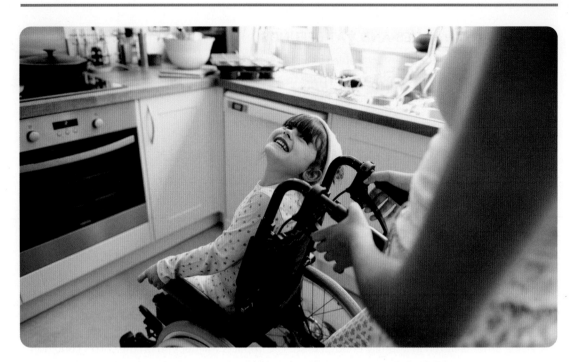

Having a child with additional needs impacts the whole family.

17.5 THE IMPACT ON SIBLINGS

Having a brother or sister with an additional need can make a sibling empathetic and caring and can bring out lots of positive qualities in a person. However, a sibling can also make sacrifices that another child of the same age is not expected to make. A sibling can sometimes feel forgotten because all the parents' attention may go to the child with additional needs. Siblings can go through an emotional journey when living with a child with additional needs, including denial and anger. They may be in denial that there is something wrong with their sibling and may question the diagnosis; they can experience anger that life has changed for them too as a result of their sibling's diagnosis. Siblings may have to sacrifice many things including receiving time and attention from their parents, spending time on their own activities and hobbies, time with friends, holidays, trips to restaurants, shopping trips, not wanting to ask for anything for fear they will be a financial burden, feelings of always living in the shadow of the child with additional needs. Siblings may worry about the future of the child with additional needs, particularly as their parents get older.

The impact to their everyday life will depend on the severity of the additional need that their brother/sister has. For siblings living with a child with severe autism, even having a friend over can be challenging. Siblings can sometimes be expected to give parents a break and take on the role of the carer. This can be rewarding, but if it happens too often it can be draining on the siblings. If a family has financial worries as a result of a parent giving up work to care for a child with additional needs, this also impacts a sibling. Siblings may become much more independent than their peers as a result of having a sibling with additional needs as they will learn to do more for themselves because a parent may be otherwise occupied. Siblings need to be looked after too, however, and may need a break. They will also need time to be with their parents doing 'normal' things, like trips to the cinema, restaurants, shopping centres, etc. Siblings need to learn to express their feelings and emotions and try to be open and honest with their families as it can be a stressful environment at times to live with a child with an additional need.

> ### REFLECTIVE PRACTICE
>
> Think about the everyday things in your life that might be impacted by having a child with additional needs in your family.

17.6 SUPPORT GROUPS AND VOLUNTARY SERVICES

Many voluntary organisations have been set up to provide support for children with additional needs and their families. Some of these organisations are run on a completely voluntary basis and rely totally on the public for donations, while others receive substantial government funding, but usually need to raise additional funding themselves. Most organisations have a website outlining their role and the services they provide.

> ### Extend your learning
>
> Research voluntary organisations in your area that support families and children with additional needs.

DOWN SYNDROME IRELAND

Down Syndrome Ireland provide support and services to people with Down syndrome and their families through a national office and 25 branches nationwide. They provide 'all through life' supports to people with Down syndrome and their families across Ireland with specialists in the areas of  health, speech and language, early development, education and adult education and independence. Their services enhance the lives of thousands of children and adults with Down syndrome. Some of the supports they provide include:

* Parent support groups
* Sports and fitness classes
* Speech and language therapy services
* Mother and toddler play sessions
* Information talks/expert speakers
* Occupational therapy services

* Counselling
* Social outings
* Summer camp
* Music therapy
* Lámh classes

AUTISM ASSISTANCE DOGS IRELAND

Autism Assistance Dogs Ireland are committed to raising autism awareness, understanding and inclusion within the community. Their primary focus is to train and place highly skilled autism assistance dogs. Assistance dogs are trained to the highest international standards to provide safety to children in public places. Assistance dogs enable children to go out and about safely. They reduce anxiety not just for the child but for the whole family. They can be a lifeline for children and their families when a child is suffering from the sometimes-debilitating symptoms of autism.

Assistance dogs can prove an invaluable asset to a child with autism and their family.

Below is a case study that can be found on their website at: https://www.autismassistancedogsireland.ie/about-us/case-studies

EDEL SHAW, JACK'S MUM:

'Before Thorpe and Autism Assistance Dogs came into our lives, life was chaotic. We lived a very isolated life, going nowhere as a family. If we needed to go anywhere, either myself or Dermot would stay at home with Jack, and the other would go out with our other son, Oisin. Jack is a notorious bolter, and worse still, a bolter who loves water and has no understanding of danger. Once he left the small toddler stage life was horrific, just horrific. He would get out into the middle of roads, running up the white lines with cars flying past on either side as I ran after him to try and save him. We have had many genuine near-death experiences. Since Autism Assistance Dogs rang to say that Jack was to get Thorpe, she has just changed our world. It is extraordinary on so many levels. Jack is calm, less anxious, he feels safe. Thorpe has helped so much. We are now willing to try new things. Of course the big things are great, but the ability to walk down the main street, the simple things that other families take for granted, without fearing the worst for your child, without having to try and deal with the 'tutter brigade', those who make the comments – this has been huge. People now see Jack with Thorpe and they make allowances for him. They understand.'

Collaborate

Discuss as a class the impact of Jack's additional needs on his family under the following headings:

* Financial
* Emotional/social
* Physical
* Siblings

Now discuss how the introduction of Thorpe changed family life under the same headings.

SHOW YOU KNOW

1. Explain your understanding of the Domiciliary Care Allowance.

2. Why might someone be entitled to receive a Carer's Allowance?

3. What services can someone access with a medical card?

4. What are the main emotional impacts to a family when their child is diagnosed with an additional need?

5. What supports will siblings need?

Section 6

Reflective Practice

Engaging in Reflective Practice

18.1 INTRODUCTION

This chapter will focus on the importance of reflective practice when working with children with additional needs in an early years setting. Research indicates that reflective practice is the key to personal and professional learning and development. Research also shows a positive relationship between professionals who engage in reflective practice and positive outcomes for children.

18.2 WHAT IS REFLECTIVE PRACTICE?

Reflection is the process of reviewing and evaluating your practice. It is essential for the ELC practitioner to engage in reflection, as through reflection an ELC practitioner can make better sense of their role and all aspects of the ELC setting. Reflection is a key element of both Síolta and Aistear. According to Aistear (2009), 'Reflective practice involves adults thinking about their work with children and planning and implementing the curriculum to best support the children's interests and strengths. Observing, listening and discussing with colleagues are key components of reflective practice.' Aistear's principle on relevant and meaningful experiences refers to the adult's ability to reflect on practice. Ongoing assessment of what children do, say and make, and reflection on these experiences helps practitioners to plan more developmentally appropriate and meaningful learning experiences for children. This also enables them to improve their practice (Aistear, 2009, p. 11).

18.3 HOW TO ENGAGE IN REFLECTIVE PRACTICE

Reflective practice requires the ELC practitioner to reflect, review and evaluate their practice. ELC practitioners need to engage in reflective practice regularly. It enables you to analyse previous activities and improve and develop them, making them more challenging. When working with children with additional needs, every day will be different: some days will be rewarding while other days will be challenging. In order to learn from both the good days and the bad, the key is to reflect on your practice.

To reflect, practitioners need to be able to:

* Have time and space to think.

* Have regular individual review and appraisal meetings.

* Be given time to observe the activities of the day in an objective manner.

* Collaborate with colleagues and other professionals.

* Ask reflective questions.

Effective ELC practitioners will reflect on their thoughts and actions in relation to their practice. To work with children with additional needs an ELC practitioner needs to be open to learning and to improving their practice. Reflective questions that an ELC practitioner may ask themselves include:

* How will I improve my practice?
* How will I evaluate it?
* What went well?
* What needs to be improved?
* What resources do I need?
* Who can help me?
* Where can I learn more about this?
* Where can I see other practitioners doing this?
* Who will support me to do this?

Reflection is a learning process. It helps an ELC practitioner to learn more about their practice, the children they are educating and caring for, and the parents and families they are supporting. Being a reflective practitioner helps to make an ELC practitioner a more effective one.

Pollard (2002) has identified the following seven characteristics of reflective practice as useful in helping ELC practitioners gain a collective understanding of what reflective practice involves and how it can improve child outcomes:

1. An active focus on goals, how these might be addressed and the potential consequences of these.

2. A commitment to a continuous cycle of monitoring practice, evaluating and revisiting it.

3. A focus on informed judgements about practice, based on evidence.

4. Open-minded, responsive and inclusive attitudes.

5. The capacity to reframe one's own practice in light of evidence-based reflections and insights based on research.

6. Dialogue with other colleagues, in-house and with external networks.

7. The capacity to mediate and adapt from externally developed frameworks, making informed judgements and defending or challenging existing practice.

(Pollard. A., p. 8)

Reflective practice in the ELC setting is influenced by action research, which aims to bring about positive change in order to better respond to the needs of children and families. This process relies on critical reflection, where professionals question their own assumptions about children and their work with children.

18.4 WHY ENGAGE IN REFLECTIVE PRACTICE?

Reflective practice allows ELC practitioners to challenge their own values and attitudes, beliefs and assumptions. This is particularly important when working with children with additional needs, as all children are unique and individual but sometimes people can paint all children with additional needs with the same brush. For example, although children with Down syndrome share common characteristics related to their condition, they still have their own personalities, likes and dislikes. Therefore, each child will have different levels of need in the ELC setting.

The terminology used around additional needs is changing all the time and becoming more inclusive. A child is a child, before any label or diagnosis, and should be referred to as a child and not their diagnosis, i.e. a child with Downs syndrome, not a Down syndrome child. They are children, first and foremost, and their needs must be met in the same professional way as those of any other child in an ELC setting. Research indicates that children learn the most when ELC practitioners reflect on their own values and consider how their views of children and childhood impact on their practice.

When working with children with additional needs a good partnership with parents/guardians is of the upmost importance. ELC practitioners must always keep their relationships with parents/guardians professional. Interactions with parents/guardians are always good opportunities to learn as the parents will have a wealth of knowledge about their child.

18.5 REFLECTING ON YOUR ROLE

In reflecting on your practice, you will be reflecting upon your role also, your perception of it and how others perceive it. Think about:

* How do you want others to see you?
* How do parents perceive you?
* How do the ELC team view you?
* What kind of practitioner are you?
* What kind of practitioner do you want to be?

To be able to answer these questions, you will have to understand yourself both professionally and personally. When working with children with additional needs, you need to know the child and their needs; you need to be able to ensure you are inclusive in your practice; you need to be able to manage change effectively; have the ability to work as part of a team; work in partnership with parents and families; have a good understanding of child development; have effective communication and interpersonal skills; support the child's learning and development; be able to plan for, extend and intervene, where appropriate, in babies' and young children's learning and work with the multidisciplinary team.

REFLECTIVE PRACTICE

Think of a recent activity that you planned and carried out with children while on professional practice placement. Ask yourself:

* What worked well? How and why did it work?
* What was the impact on outcomes for the children?
* What didn't work and why?
* How could it have been improved?

18.6 REFLECTIVE PRACTICE IN THE IRISH CONTEXT

Our two national frameworks, Síolta (2006) and Aistear (2009), both incorporate the importance of reflective practice.

SÍOLTA AND REFLECTIVE PRACTICE

Síolta proposes that quality early childhood practice is built upon the unique role of the adult. The competencies, qualifications, dispositions and experience of adults, in addition to their capacity to reflect upon their role, are essential components in supporting and ensuring quality experiences for each child. Standard 11 Professional Practice states: 'Practising in a professional manner requires that individuals have skills, knowledge, values and attitudes appropriate to their role and responsibility within the setting. In addition, it requires regular reflection upon practice and engagement in supported, ongoing professional development (Síolta Research Digest Standard 11 Professional Practice). Síolta recommends that services support and promote regular opportunities for practitioners to reflect upon and review their practice and contribute positively to the development of quality practice in the setting.

AISTEAR AND REFLECTIVE PRACTICE

Aistear proposes that the role of the adult in early childhood is central because adults enhance learning through a respectful understanding of the child's uniqueness. Early learning takes place through a reciprocal relationship between the adult and the child; sometimes the adult leads the learning, and at other times the child leads. The adult alters the type and amount of support as the child grows in confidence and competence and achieves new things (NCCA, 2009). Ongoing observation and assessment of what children do, say and make, and reflection on these experiences, enables practitioners to plan more developmentally appropriate and meaningful learning experiences for children. This also enables practitioners to improve their own practice. The need to engage in reflective practice is a key message from the Aistear framework. This message is further developed in the Aistear Síolta Practice Guide (see http://aistearsiolta.ie).

AISTEAR SÍOLTA PRACTICE GUIDE

The Aistear Síolta Practice Guide was developed in 2015 by the National Council for Curriculum and Assessment (NCCA) to support professionals to work with Aistear and Síolta together. It includes examples of quality practice along with self-assessment tools and templates that support reflection and analysis of professional practice (see Section 2 of that guide). As already noted, the practitioner's role is fundamental in supporting all children to learn and develop to their full potential. However, the demands of this role can often be overlooked or misunderstood by parents, other professionals, the community and wider society. The way in which practitioners view, describe and explain their role impacts on how it is seen by others. This image and sense of identity as a professional can, in turn, influence how practitioners feel about their own role, carry out their daily work with children and interact with parents and other professionals.

18.7 MODELS OF REFLECTIVE PRACTICE

GIBBS' REFLECTIVE CYCLE

In order to use Gibbs' Reflective Cycle, when working with children with additional needs, reflect on an event/activity/incident that involved the child and you, the practitioner.

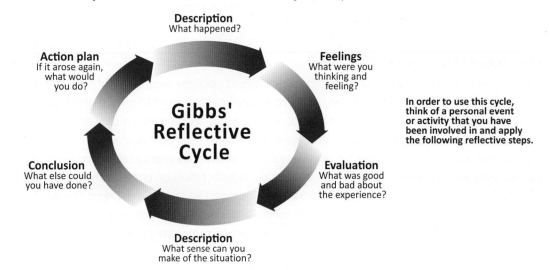

In order to use this cycle, think of a personal event or activity that you have been involved in and apply the following reflective steps.

STEP 1: DESCRIPTION

During this step, you describe the event in detail, without drawing any immediate conclusions. The most common questions that can help create an objective description are:

* What happened?

* When did it happen?

* Where did it happen?

* Who was involved?

* What did I do myself?

* What did other people do?

* What was the result of these actions?

All details of the event are vital, including why other people were involved and their role, as this will provide a better understanding of what happened. The practitioner needs to be as objective as possible and provide all the details of the event. It is important to not leave out any information. Think of it like a jigsaw puzzle: if one piece of information is missing, you can't complete the jigsaw!

STEP 2: FEELINGS

This phase is about the feelings that the event triggered, as well as what your thoughts were, as described in Step 1. The intention is not to discuss the feelings in detail or comment on them directly. Emotions do not need to be evaluated or judged at this stage. Awareness is the most critical goal of this phase. Helpful questions include:

* What did I feel leading up to the event?

* What did I feel during the event?

* What did I feel after the event?

* How do I look back on this event?

* What do I think other people felt during the event?

* How do I think others feel about the event now?

Because people often have difficulty talking about their feelings, it helps that they are encouraged by the questions or someone asking these questions. This also demonstrates that Gibbs' Reflective Cycle can be used in an individual setting or in a mentoring or supervision setting. The final two questions also allow one to see the event from other people's perspectives.

STEP 3: EVALUATION

In this step, ask yourself whether the experience of the event in Step 1 was good or bad. Which approach worked well and why? Which approach did not work as well and why? It can be difficult for people to be objective about an event. To conduct a proper evaluation, the following questions may be helpful:

* What went well during the event?

* Why was that?

* What did not go so well?

* Why was that?

* What was my contribution?

* What contribution did other people make?

It is worth evaluating good and bad experiences. The subsequent steps in this Reflective Cycle help people learn from such experiences.

STEP 4: ANALYSIS

This analysis is often done alongside Step 3 and concerns what you have learned from the event. Because of the experience, you now know what to do in similar future situations. This means that both positive and negative things and/or problems you experienced will be written down and analysed individually. People with a growth mindset often learn more when things go wrong. This stage is an important learning tool when working with children with additional needs as it helps you to approach similar situations in future with a greater understanding of what works to support the child.

STEP 5: CONCLUSION

Here you take a step back and look at yourself from a distance, asking what else you could have done during the event. The information gathered earlier is very valuable in this step and can encourage you to come to a useful conclusion. The following questions may be helpful:

* To what positive experience did the event lead?

* To what negative experience did the event lead?

* What would I do differently if the event were to happen again in the future?

* Which skills do I need to develop for a similar event in the future?

STEP 6: ACTION PLAN

In this final step, actions are developed for future events. Based on the conclusions reached in Step 5, people make concrete promises to themselves. The intention is to keep these promises. If everything went well, you could promise yourself to act in the same way the next time. In areas where things did not go well, you can promise yourself not to make the same mistakes again, asking yourself what a more effective approach would be and which change will lead to actual improvement. In addition to an action plan, it is wise to plan on how to encourage yourself to stick to these promises. You could also include your action plans as part of the child's Individual Education Plan (IEP)

(Adapted from What is Gibbs' Reflective Cycle?:
https://www.toolshero.com/management/gibbsreflective-cycle-graham-gibbs/)

Reflecting on your own experiences when working with children with additional needs can help a practitioner to do things differently, try new approaches and perform better in future. As the above shows, these experiences do not have to be positive; negative experiences are also helpful. Gibbs' Reflective Cycle stimulates you to think long and hard about how to do things better next time – the core of reflective practice. People do not simply learn to understand certain events better but also learn to judge how the same event can be handled in different ways in the future.

Collaborate

In small groups, read the following case study and devise a template based on Gibbs' Reflective Cycle that you could use to reflect on Aoife's experience. Adapt the template as required based on your own experiences of working with children with additional needs.

CASE STUDY

Aoife was completing her work placement in a preschool that had two non-verbal children attending. She planned an activity that involved using puppets for the children. She obtained teddies that made sounds for the two non-verbal children, but on the day of the planned activity she forgot to bring these teddies with her. The other children used the puppets and had a 'show', and although the two children who were non-verbal each held a puppet, they did not partake. Aoife felt terrible that the activity was not as inclusive as she had originally planned it to be. She felt like she had let both the children and the placement down.

KOLB'S EXPERIENTIAL LEARNING CYCLE

Kolb's Experiential Learning Cycle emphasises the central role that experience plays in the learning process. Just as Jean Piaget proposed that children are active agents in their own learning, Kolb's model proposes that adults are active agents in their own learning. This learning cycle involves four stages.

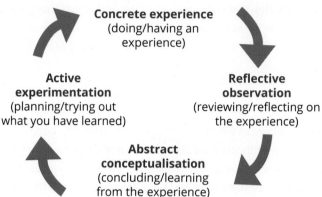

Concrete experience
(doing/having an experience)

Reflective observation
(reviewing/reflecting on the experience)

Abstract conceptualisation
(concluding/learning from the experience)

Active experimentation
(planning/trying out what you have learned)

STAGE 1

The cycle begins with a concrete experience as a result of doing something.

STAGE 2

The second stage, reflective observation, means taking time out from 'doing', stepping back from the task and reviewing what has been done and experienced. At this point, lots of questions can be asked of self and others as to how the experience went.

STAGE 3

The third stage, abstract conceptualisation, is the process of making sense of what has happened and interpreting the activity or event based on whether or not you were satisfied with the outcome.

STAGE 4

The final stage, active experimentation, is where the learner considers how they are going to put what they have learned into practice. If everything went well, it may mean refining the activity/event to make it even better; if things did not go well, this is the time to plan how you will undertake the activity/event in the future to try to improve the outcome.

In summary, three elements are central to Kolb's model:

1. Emphasis is on the 'here and now' of concrete experiences.

2. Ideas are not fixed and unchangeable but are formed and re-formed again through reflecting on experiences.

3. Feedback from experienced practitioners and your placement supervisor can provide the basis for continuous learning and further evaluation of your work.

Kolb's Learning Cycle is again very relevant to working with children with additional needs. Every day and every child can be different; continuously learning from your experiences and from others will ensure the best outcomes for yourself and the children you are working with.

SCHÖN'S REFLECTIVE MODEL

Another approach is the work of Donald Schön. Schön (1991) distinguishes between 'reflection in action' and 'reflection on action'.

REFLECTION **IN** ACTION

Reflecting as something happens
* Consider the situation
* Decide how to act
* Act immediately

REFLECTION **ON** ACTION

Reflecting after something happens
* Reconsider the situation
* Think about what needs changing for the future

'Reflection in action' is reflection during the 'doing' stage; that is, reflecting on the incident while it can still benefit your learning. This is carried out during an activity/event rather than after the event when you might reflect on how you would do things differently in the future. This is an efficient method of reflection as it allows you to react and change an incident/event at the time it happens.

For example, you may be reading a story to the children and you can see they are not as interested as you would like them to be. Your reflection in action may prompt you to make the story more appealing to the children by changing your voice for the various characters in the book, which may help the children pay more attention.

At the end of the storytelling, you may reflect again on whether or not your strategy worked. This is called 'reflection on action'. Based on this, you may decide to rehearse how you will read the story and think of how props can also be used to further sustain the children's interest.

18.8 REFLECTIVE PRACTICE IN ELC

Reflective practice is not just a personal task that you carry out on yourself. In the ELC setting it involves much more:

* Observing more experienced peers.
* Listening to and observing babies, toddlers and young children.
* Observing family members and their interactions with children and staff in ELC.
* Learning from supervision while on professional practice placement.
* Peer mentoring.
* Using a reflective journal.
* Reflecting in practice as well as on practice.

OBSERVING MORE EXPERIENCED PRACTITIONERS

Observing practitioners working with children with additional needs is key to learning and developing your practice. Professional practice placement is a fantastic opportunity to learn more about children with additional needs. Academic learning is only one part of your journey to becoming a qualified ELC practitioner; the placement element is usually the most enjoyable part of the course for many learners. Observing and learning from more experienced practitioners is central to your professional development. Some of these practitioners will have worked in ELC for several years and may display a level of expertise in their work from which you can learn, and which can support you in bringing your academic learning to life in a positive way for you and the children.

WORKING WITH BABIES, TODDLERS AND YOUNG CHILDREN

Feeling welcome and having a sense of belonging is important for all children in the ELC setting. The term 'inclusion' does not just apply to children with additional needs, but has a much broader meaning and applies to all aspects of the ELC setting: the practices, attitudes and, above all, the values that create the ELC environment that make everyone feel comfortable. Inclusion has many meanings for the babies, toddlers and young children that attend a setting from the sense of belonging to the room that they attend, and the feeling that they are part of the whole setting community. Their needs, personalities and individuality all need to be catered for. The setting can ensure babies, toddlers and young children with additional needs feel included in the setting by planning the curriculum with their needs in mind and having positive interactions.

Some ideas for promoting inclusion include:

* Displaying all children's work.

* Encouraging all children to be independent.

* Providing for choices.

* Listening to babies, toddlers and young children.

* Allowing children freedom to express themselves.

* Giving the child a voice.

Supporting children's access and participation in the early years setting is the key intention of the access and inclusion model (AIM). The Section "My Inclusion Plan" supports the child with additional needs to have meaningful participation in the ELC setting. Reflection is key to the success of the plan for the child.

WORKING WITH PARENTS/GUARDIANS

Building partnerships with parents is particularly important to support the child with additional needs in an ELC setting, and by using reflective practice we learn from both observing parents interacting with their children and by having supportive, meaningful relationships with the parents. When parents and practitioners work together the outcome is always better for children. Aistear's *Guidelines for Good Practice* examines the benefits to good partnership. Practitioners should use reflective practice to learn from their interactions and experiences with parents.

The benefits of parents and practitioners working together

Parents	Practitioners	Children
▪ feel valued and respected ▪ are more involved in their children's learning and development ▪ can share information about their children ▪ feel their family's values, practices, traditions and beliefs are understood and taken into account ▪ feel comfortable visiting the setting, talking to and planning with practitioners ▪ know more about their children's experiences outside the home and use this information to support their learning and development more effectively ▪ understand why early childhood care and education is important ▪ have increased confidence in their own parenting skills.	▪ understand better the children and families in their settings and use this information to make learning more enjoyable and rewarding for all children ▪ can help children develop a sense of identity and belonging in the setting by actively engaging with and finding out about family values, traditions and beliefs, and building on these where appropriate ▪ benefit from parents' skills and expertise ▪ can provide a more emotionally secure environment for children.	▪ feel more secure and benefit more from the educational opportunities given to them ▪ move from one setting to another with greater confidence ▪ see learning as more enjoyable when their home life is 'visible' in the setting ▪ enjoy hearing and seeing their home language in the setting when their home language is neither English nor Irish ▪ experience more connections between the different services that support them.

(Aistear, *Guidelines for Good Practice*, p. 8)

LEARNING FROM SUPERVISION WHILE ON PROFESSIONAL PRACTICE PLACEMENT

As part of your professional practice placement, you will have regular supervision with your supervisor to support you in your work. This one-to-one support is a valuable method of promoting effective practice. This is a specially dedicated time for the supervisor to support and listen to you, which in turn enables you to continuously improve your practice. It provides you with an opportunity to reflect on your practice and explore any worries or concerns you may have and contributes to you developing confidence and competence in your work. It is important that you contribute to these sessions by keeping a journal of the areas you wish to discuss and to seek advice for areas of concern you may have. We can all learn by asking questions, particularly when working with children with additional needs since every day is a new learning experience. A suitable time and date for your meeting should be agreed in advance as this ensures you are prepared for the meeting. Meetings should be documented and referred to regularly to reflect on continuing professional development.

PEER MENTORING

Peer mentoring in ELC involves learning from the practitioners you encounter daily in your placement/s and from other students, both on your course and in your placement/s. Whether in a baby room, toddler room or pre-school room, the staff you work with will provide you with valuable learning opportunities as you observe, reflect on and learn from their work practices. Different practitioners and ELC settings will have different approaches to working with children with additional needs, and group discussions allow students to learn from each other, reflect on their experiences and use reflective practice to think about how they might deal with situations that may arise. In this way, possible solutions can be found if you experience difficulties in your service. The following are some peer reflection activities that can be completed on a regular basis using the model of reflective practice chosen by the college/centre.

REFLECTIVE LEARNING JOURNAL

Many ELC courses will require learners to present a reflective learning journal as part of their assessment. This journal could include:

1. Reflection on the daily timetable/routines. Would you change anything?

2. Reflection on Aistear/ Síolta in action.

3. Reflection on communication and teamwork in the setting.

4. Reflection on your supervision experience.

5. Reflection on your own personal learning and development.

The evidence for each entry will include a reflection using the stages of a chosen model of reflective practice.

The structure of a reflective learning journal is flexible, and you can be creative and take an approach that suits your style. However, reflective writing should include an examination of the following:

1. Description of the task.

2. The learner's feelings, attitudes and values.

3. The key learning that took place.

4. Changes as a result of the reflection.

1. Description of the task

Consider these two descriptions of the one task by the same practitioner.

Description 1: I set up cornflour and water in the water play area with the intention of making gloop with four children. I invited the children to come to the water play area. I explained to the children we were going to make gloop. I gave the children the jugs with the cornflour and water in them, and invited them to pour them out and mix them together. The child with additional needs started screaming.

Description 2: I set up the water play area with the intention of making gloop with four children. I was not sure whether TC1 would like the gloop as they do not like change and they may have been confused that there was not water in the water container. When the children approached and saw there was no water in the water container, they all started asking questions all together and one child walked away. The child with additional needs started screaming and was distressed. This made me panic that the activity would not work out. I explained to the children that they needed to pour the containers out and mix the contents together. I demonstrated to the children how to make the gloop. The children started to mix the cornflour and water together and reacting to the sensation of the gloop in their hands. The child with additional needs poked the gloop that one of their friends had made and discovered they liked it.

Both descriptions of the task could have continued to include a synopsis of the activity, how the children reacted and so on. Dialogue could also have been recorded. As demonstrated in the second description, an account of feelings (subjective) can be an integral part of the recount of what happened. It does not have to stick to objective facts.

2. The learner's feelings, attitudes and values

This is where you might explain the reasons why you did what you did, the way you did it and why you were feeling the way you did. For example, considering the sample descriptions above, why was the activity set up for only four children? Perhaps the activity was planned that way; perhaps only four children were present in the room. Why was gloop selected instead of water play, with which the children are familiar? Why were the children not involved in selecting the activity? Why might there have been feelings of uncertainty as to what the children might like? Was there fear that some children would be upset, that the situation would get out of hand? Was the supervisor looking in on the activity and causing feelings of nervousness? Did another practitioner assist the child with additional needs? Description 2 demonstrates that the practitioner took control by demonstrating the activity; description 1 does not show this.

Skills of interpretation might be strengthened here by examining how child development theory might interpret the event. Did the children have choices or control? In this case, they did not. You could even analyse the activity that was chosen.

3. The key learning that took place

The following terms may be helpful prompts in considering and discussing key learning:

* Looking back …
* I now understand that …
* Having experienced …
* I now realise …

* I will need to … in future
* Faced with a similar situation in the future I would …

4. Changes as a result of the reflection

In relation to the example above, you might now understand that the practitioner was new in the placement and should have consulted more with the room supervisor at the planning stage. You might also recognise that the practitioner did not want to seem needy or lacking in confidence and wanted to showcase their skills. You might also recognise that consulting with the children about the gloop activity earlier might have made for an easier introduction to the activity. In future, the practitioner might plan to give themselves more time observing colleagues before embarking on an activity. They might consider taking on activities about which they feel very confident in order to allow time for their confidence to grow in other areas. As noted in chapter 1, writing takes practice, and reflective writing is no different. It is good practice to take a few minutes at the end of the day to reflect on classes: what you learned, what was interesting and why you were particularly interested, what was boring and why. Alternatively, reflect on an event outside college that you did or did not enjoy. When doing your reflective journal for your assessment tasks, take notes at each stage of the activity or event, from planning to afterwards. It may not all be used, but it will help you to reflect on what actually happened. Even a few hours after an event, things are seen and remembered differently and consequently interpreted differently. It is important to remember that, irrespective of assessment, reflection now and throughout your career is essential to your continued growth as a professional.

SHOW YOU KNOW

1. Define what reflective practice means.
2. What does reflective practice look like in the Irish context?
3. Discuss three models of reflective practice.
4. Describe two ways a student could use reflective practice.

Professional and Personal Supports for Early Years Practitioners Working with Children with Additional Needs

What I will learn:

* Explore what personal and professional development is.
* Look at what personal supports are available.
* Examine what professional supports are available to ELC practitioners in the Irish context.

19.1 INTRODUCTION

'The role of the adult in supporting quality early childhood experiences for young children is absolutely central' (Síolta Research Digest, 2004, p. 2). However, in order to be a positive role model for the children for whose care and education they are responsible, early years practitioners will need professional and personal supports. This should not be underestimated. Working with children with additional needs in an ELC setting requires a practitioner to be willing to engage in professional development, e.g. if working with a child with epilepsy, you would need training on how to administer the child's medication. 'Practising in a professional manner requires that individuals have skills, knowledge, values and attitudes appropriate to their role and responsibility within the setting. In addition, it requires regular reflection upon practice and engagement in supported, ongoing professional development'. (Síolta, 2006.)

19.2 PERSONAL AND PROFESSIONAL DEVELOPMENT

Effective personal and professional development involves ensuring that you have the knowledge and understanding at the highest level possible when working with children, including children with additional needs. Professional development is the acquisition of skills and knowledge for career advancement, but there should also be an element of personal development. In light of the current policy context, early childhood educators are required to have a complex understanding of child development and early education issues and provide rich, meaningful educational experiences for all children and families in their care.

When working with children, our personal qualities and skills are as important as our theoretical knowledge and professional skills. Personal development and professional development are equally important. This is particularly true when working with children with additional needs in an ELC setting as the child's needs and the environment are constantly changing. The professional skills and knowledge that you acquire through studying and professional work practice placement and how they are incorporated into your practice is very much influenced by your values and beliefs. Both Síolta and Aistear highlight the importance of the ELC practitioner's role in ensuring quality early childhood learning experiences for young children. 'Early learning takes place through a reciprocal relationship between the adult and the child – sometimes the adult leads the learning and sometimes the child leads. The adult enhances learning through a respectful understanding of the child's uniqueness. He/she alters the type and amount of support as the child grows in confidence and competence and achieves new things, (NCCA, 2009, p. 9).

This principle highlights how significant and beneficial the adult's relationship with the child can be; to enhance the development of this relationship the adult must be very aware of their own personal and professional competencies.

Personal and professional development is an integral part of the lifelong learning process. The effectiveness of our personal and professional development depends largely on our desire to grow and develop as a person. Receiving both personal and professional support when working in an ELC setting with children with additional needs is central to ensuring that the ELC practitioner continues to offer a quality experience for the child. Personal supports can take many forms but centre around the wellbeing of the practitioner. Professional supports are assistance provided to improve the skills, qualities, training and qualifications of an ELC practitioner.

19.3 PERSONAL SUPPORTS FOR EARLY YEARS PRACTITIONERS

Early years practitioners are always concerned about the wellbeing of the children in their care but should be mindful that their own wellbeing is also important. We all matter! ELC practitioners are important role models to the children they work with and therefore should have positive attitudes to healthy behaviours and have positive outlooks on learning and life.

Mindfulness is a process of intentionally bringing our attention to what is happening in the present moment with acceptance and openness. It means being curious and not judging our feelings or experiences. Caring for young children and children with additional needs can be stressful. ELC practitioners nurture, teach, prepare meals, assist with toileting, change nappies, play, resolve conflicts and provide the structure that helps children feel safe and secure. But the pay isn't great and the hours are long. Early childhood professionals have to be the world's best multitaskers, juggling everything from nappy changes to school readiness, from parent meetings to lullabies. It can be a stressful job so it is important to look after your mental and physical health. Mindfulness can help reduce stress. Regular mindfulness practice has been shown to reduce both emotional and physical distress (e.g. anxiety, depression and pain) and to decrease the effects of traumatic events (such as family violence or childhood abuse). Mindfulness training may also protect against burnout and compassion fatigue for professionals in social service work. Using the STOP strategy may help in the heat of the moment:

* **S**top. Pause and focus.

* **T**ake a deep breath in and out. Notice how it feels to breathe.

* **O**bserve. Acknowledge what is happening, positive or negative, inside you or outside. Let go of judgement and simply note your feelings and responses.

* **P**roceed. You've given yourself the space to think about the way you want to respond. By avoiding a cycle of anger and blame, you allow yourself to be present in the moment and walk to the door with a smile, offering this child and parent a calm, nurturing transition.

REFLECTIVE PRACTICE

It's 9:30 a.m., and most of the children in the pre-school are settled in. Everyone is busy playing at the different stations you and the team had set up before the children arrived, but you are preparing to transition to the morning story. Suddenly, a parent bursts through the door with her son, who has autism, in tow. He's crying and clinging to her for dear life. She is shouting about an incident that she claims happened the previous day. The other children have stopped what they are doing and are all watching now.

What steps do you take to deal with this situation?

TIPS FOR SUPPORTING THE WELLBEING OF YOUR COLLEAGUES IN THE ELC SETTING

* Develop and be part of a work culture where everyone is treated with respect and bullying and harassment are not tolerated.

* Develop and be part of a culture where open and honest communication is encouraged. Support and mutual respect should be the norm.

* If possible, give ELC practitioners more control over their work and how they do it.

* Ensure ELC practitioners have the correct level of skills for the job they are required to do.

* Ensure that the team has a manageable workload.

* Where possible, create flexible working hours to try and support a work–life harmony.

* Audit the work environment for physical stressors and try to eliminate them, e.g. poor lighting.

19.4 PROFESSIONAL SUPPORTS FOR EARLY YEARS PRACTITIONERS

In every working environment people need professional supports to help them to do their job, and working with children with additional needs in an ELC setting is no different. Continuous Professional Development (CPD) is the term used to describe learning activities that professionals engage in to develop and enhance their abilities. CPD can take the form of in-house training, or training which takes place outside the organisation.

Many people tend to focus on formal training, but CPD encompasses any form of activities from which you learn and develop. This can, therefore, include elearning, case discussions and reading, but can also be as simple as sharing knowledge and challenges with colleagues.

Hynes (2009) and French (2013) highlight one of the key challenges with developing professional practice in the early years as the lack of investment in CPD (cited by Longford Childcare Committee available at: https://longfordchildcare.ie/professional-practice-early-years/.) Despite the challenges lots of ELC practitioners see the value in completing professional development and, in recent years, more professional development courses have come on stream for ELC practitioners working in the Irish context.

The benefits of completing professional development courses include:

1. Keeping pace with the standards of others in the same field.

2. Maintaining and enhancing knowledge and skills to deliver a professional service.

3. Staying up to date with changing trends.

4. Becoming more effective in the workplace.

5. Staying interested in your profession.

6. Gaining access to experts in the fields.

There are many organisations that provide professional supports to ELC practitioners. Some provide more general learning to work with young children and some are more specific to working with particular conditions but, rest assured, there is plenty of support available: you just need to find it. Working with a child with a condition that is new to you can be challenging but it is worthwhile exploring the available supports, as the benefits for the ELC team, the child and their parents will be invaluable.

TUSLA QUALITY AND REGULATORY FRAMEWORK ELEARNING PROGRAMME

Tusla have developed a quality and regulatory framework elearning programme. It was developed following consultation with the early years sector in relation to the supports required to comply with the Childcare Act 1991 (Early Years Services) Regulations 2016. The Quality and Regulatory Framework elearning Programme is an additional support to the Quality and Regulatory Framework document. The aim of this programme is to:

* Assist registered providers and staff of early years services to prepare for a Tusla early years inspection.

* Support early years professionals to meet the requirements of the Child Care Act 1991 (Early Years Services) Regulations 2016 and the Childcare Act 1991 (Early Years Services) (Amendment) Regulations 2016.

The elearning programme may be used as a resource by other professionals in the early years sector; it identifies what quality early years provision looks like in practice and, as such, may also be of interest to parents and guardians. More information is available at: https://www.tusla.ie/services/preschool-services/tusla-quality-and-regulatory-framework-elearning-programme/.

FIRST 5

A key objective of First 5 is to improve Continuous Professional Development (CPD) for all those who work in early learning and care and school-age childcare settings. First 5 offer a range of courses for ELC practitioners, including long and short courses. More information is available at:
https://first5.gov.ie/practitioners/continuing-professional-development.

BETTER START

Better Start National Early Years Quality Development is a national initiative established by the Department of Children, Equality, Disability, Integration and Youth and hosted by Pobal. Better Start promotes quality and inclusion in ELC settings for children from birth to six years of age in Ireland. It provides a number of training programmes suitable for ELC practitioners as well as other useful resources to promote an inclusive environment for children with additional needs. More information can be found on: https://www.betterstart.ie/.

COUNTY CHILDCARE COMMITTEE

All the County Childcare Committees (CCC) offer supports and advice to ELC services. A key role of the CCCs is to facilitate and support the development of quality, accessible early learning and care and school-age childcare services for the overall benefit of children and their parents by taking a child-centred and partnership approach. Information about CCCs can be found at: https://myccc.ie/.

EARLY CHILDHOOD IRELAND

Early Childhood Ireland is the leading membership organisation in the early years sector. They support over 3,800 members who, in turn, support over 120,000 children across a range of service provision in Ireland. Their work includes quality enhancement, communications and publications, advocacy, training and support and information for their members. More information about their training programmes can be found on their website: https://www.earlychildhoodireland.ie/learning-hub/.

OTHER ORGANISATIONS

Many voluntary organisations operate supports and services for children with additional needs and their families related to the condition. It is worth researching the condition in Ireland and asking parents/guardians for any contact details of organisations they may be involved in. The organisation My Support Network offers information on a range of conditions affecting children in Ireland. For more information, see: https://mysupportnetwork.ie/.

Collaborate

Individually, look up the mysupportnetwork.ie website. Choose two conditions and find out what supports are available for ELC practitioners. Share your information with your group.

SHOW YOU KNOW

1. Outline the difference between personal and professional development.

2. Describe how to deal with a challenging situation.

3. Name three organisations which provide information on training courses.

GLOSSARY

Acquired additional needs	additional needs/conditions that occur after birth and are not caused by hereditary or developmental factors but by environmental factors
ADHD (Attention deficit hyperactivity disorder)	one of the commonest childhood disorders and can continue through adolescence and adulthood. Symptoms include difficulty staying focused and paying attention, difficulty controlling behaviour and hyperactivity (overactivity)
AHT (abusive head trauma)	non-accidental head injury
AIM	access and inclusion model
Asperger's syndrome	a form of autism spectrum disorder, it is a developmental disorder whereby young people have difficulty in relating to others socially and their behaviour and thinking patterns can be rigid and repetitive
Ataxic cerebral palsy	the rarest form of cerebral palsy, often leading to difficulty with balancing, and walking with a high stepping motion on tiptoe
Autism spectrum disorder (ASD)	a term used to describe a group of neurological developmental disorders that affect how people communicate, socialise and interact with others. It may also be characterised by restrictive, repetitive behaviours, interests and activities
Bacterial meningitis	bacterial infection that causes an inflammation or swelling of the membranes that surround and protect the brain and spinal cord
Cerebral palsy (CP)	an umbrella term used to refer to a group of complicated conditions that affect movement and posture because of damage to or failure in the development of the part of the brain that controls movement
Chorioamnionitis	a complication that occurs during pregnancy whereby a maternal bacterial infection travels up to the uterus and infects the amniotic fluid and foetal membranes

Chromosomes	a structure found inside the nucleus of a cell made up of proteins and DNA organised into genes
Complex multifactorial inheritance (polygenic inheritance)	Complex multifactorial gene inheritance disorders occur when more than one factor causes a trait or health problem
Conductive impairment	occurs when sound is blocked from entering the inner ear, causing hearing impairment
Congenital additional needs	additional needs present from birth
Congenital blindness	blindness from birth
Congenital cataracts	present at birth and cause a clouding of the lens of the eye
Cortical visual impairment	may cause total or partial blindness
Curriculum	refers to all learning experiences, whether formal or informal, planned or unplanned, which contribute to a child's development (NCCA, 2004)
Cystic fibrosis (CF)	a genetically inherited condition that causes one or more of the glands of the body to produce a thick, sticky mucus that affects organ function
DCD (Developmental Coordination Disorder)	also known simply as dyspraxia, affects fine and/or gross motor skills coordination
Diabetes mellitus	a lifelong condition caused by a lack of, or insufficiency of, insulin
DNA (deoxyribonucleic acid)	the chemical name for the molecule that carries genetic instructions in all living things
Down's syndrome	a complex additional need that can impact on several aspects of a child's development
Dyscalculia	a specific learning disability whereby the child (and later adult) has an innate difficulty in learning or comprehending mathematics
Dysgraphia	a learning disability that primarily affects the child's fine motor skills. Usually not diagnosed until the child is in school and demonstrates a difficulty with handwriting

Dyslexia	a specific learning difficulty that makes it more difficult for the individual to learn to read, write and spell well, and which is unexplained in relation to his/her other abilities and educational experiences
Dyspraxia	DCD (Developmental Coordination Disorder) also known simply as dyspraxia, affects fine and/or gross motor skills coordination
Epilepsy	a neurological disorder that affects the brain and causes seizures
Extremely preterm	baby born at or before 25 weeks of pregnancy
Focal seizures (partial seizures)	a form of epilepsy that can be described as simple or complex. With focal seizures, particularly with complex focal seizures, the child may experience an aura before the seizure occurs
Foetal alcohol spectrum disorders (FASDs)	a cluster of abnormalities and problems that appear in the offspring of mothers who drink alcohol during pregnancy
Foetal macrosomia	the scientific term for a baby that is too large for safe vaginal delivery
Generalised seizures	five different types of seizure that involve both sides of the brain:
	✳ *Absence seizures*: the child will typically 'zone out' for a period of up to 30 seconds
	✳ *Atonic seizures*: there is a sudden loss of muscle tone and the child may suddenly fall or drop their head – often called a 'drop attack'
	✳ *Febrile seizures*: these seizures occur when children have a very high temperature. They are most commonly seen in children between six months and five years of age and there may be a family history of this type of seizure
	✳ *Generalised tonic-clonic seizures*: the child will lose consciousness and the body, arms and legs will flex, extend and shake
	Myoclonic seizures: this type of seizure refers to quick movements or sudden jerking of a group of muscles. These seizures tend to occur in clusters, meaning that they may occur several times a day, or for several days in a row

Genetics	the scientific study of heredity and hereditary variation
Genital herpes simplex	an incurable sexually transmitted infection caused by the herpes simplex virus (HSV) (*see* HSV)
Glaucoma	a serious eye condition that results from the excessive build-up of pressure in the fluid of the eye
GLD (general learning disability)	describes delays in development leading to a difficulty to learn, understand and do things in comparison to other children of the same age. Can range from borderline mild, mild, moderate, to severe/profound
Guardians ad Litem	independent persons appointed by the court for the duration of court proceedings relating to a child. They give the child a voice in the proceedings and advise the court in respect of the child's best interests
Hemiplegia	a form of cerebral palsy where one side of the body is affected
HIV/AIDS	a life-threatening infection (usually sexually transmitted) caused by the human immunodeficiency virus (HIV)
HSV (herpes simplex virus)	there are two types: type 1 and 2. Type 1 has been found to cause genital infection but is more commonly associated with oral herpes (cold sores). Type 2 is most commonly associated with genital infection
Hydrocephalus	literally means 'water in the head' and is caused by an accumulation of cerebrospinal fluid (CSF) within the ventricles of the brain, resulting in raised pressure inside the head
individual education plan (IEP)	a written plan prepared for a named child. It is a record of what is being agreed as 'additional to' and 'different from' the usual differentiated curriculum provision that is provided to all children in the setting
Late preterm	born between 34 and 36 completed weeks of pregnancy
Mandated person	a person who has contact with children and/or families and who, because of their qualifications, training and/or employment role, are in a key position to help protect children from harm

Moderately preterm	born between 32 and 34 weeks of pregnancy
Morphology	the grammar of a language
Muscular dystrophy (MD)	refers to a group of genetically inherited muscular diseases that weaken the muscles of the body and are characterised by progressive weakening and wasting of the muscles of the body
Neonatal abstinence syndrome (NAS)	occurs when babies are born addicted to a drug and experience withdrawal after birth
Oppositional defiant disorder (ODD)	characterised by an ongoing pattern of disobedient, hostile and defiant behaviour toward authority figures and which goes beyond the bounds of normal childhood behaviour
Organogenesis	formation of vital organs
Paraplegia	a form of cerebral palsy in which only the legs are affected
PECS board	Picture Exchange Communication Systems
Peer mentoring (in ELC)	involves learning from the practitioners you encounter daily in your placement(s) and from other students, both on your course and in your placement(s)
Phonology	the sounds of a language
Pragmatics	knowing how to use language appropriately, e.g. turn taking, tone and volume of voice in different situations, eye contact, knowing when it is appropriate to change topic
Pre-eclampsia	high blood pressure during pregnancy
Premature birth	a birth that takes place more than three weeks before the baby's estimated due date
Psoriasis	a skin disease that causes red, itchy, scaly patches, most commonly on the knees, elbows, trunk and scalp
Psychoactive drugs	drugs that act on the nervous system, causing changes to the individual's physical and mental state

Quadriplegia	the most the most severe form of cerebral palsy as all four limbs are affected
Reflection	the process of reviewing and evaluating your practice
Retinitis pigmentosa	a genetically inherited progressive eye condition whereby the photoreceptors (rods and cones) located in the retina develop abnormally
Retinopathy of prematurity (ROP)	an eye disorder that predominantly affects prematurely born babies
Semantics	the meaning of words and sentences
SENO (special educational needs organiser)	helps coordinate the formation of the IEP (individual education plan) and the school's implementation of it
Sensorineural impairment	caused by problems with the nerves connecting the inner ear to the brain (vestibulocochlear nerve or cranial nerve VIII), the inner ear itself or the areas of the brain that process sound
Septicaemia	blood poisoning
Shoulder dystocia	an emergency event that can occur suddenly during a vaginal delivery when the baby's shoulder becomes stuck while entering the birth canal, usually on the mother's pelvic bone
Single-gene inheritance	relates to abnormalities that occur in the DNA sequence of a single gene
Spina bifida	the commonest neural tube defect (NTD), causing incomplete development of the spinal cord. Different forms or types include spina bifida occulta, spina bifida meningocele, spina bifida myelomeningocele, encephalocele and anencephaly.
Syntax	word order in sentences
Syphilis	a serious sexually transmitted infection caused by the bacterium Treponema pallidum
Teratology	name given to the study of the causes of birth defects and resulting additional needs

Umbilical cord prolapse	when the umbilical cord drops down into the cervical opening in front of the baby as it enters the birth canal, occurs very rarely
UNCRC	United Nations Convention on the Rights of the Child
Uterine rupture	a very rare and serious event in which the wall or lining of the mother's uterus tears open
Very preterm	baby born at less than 32 weeks of pregnancy

REFERENCES/BIBLIOGRAPHY

AIM (2016). 'Access and Inclusion Model (AIM): Better Pre-school Access for Children with Disabilities Access and Inclusion Model.' Available from https://www.aims.ie/ [accessed 10 September 2021].

Autism Assistance Dogs Ireland (n.d.). 'Case Studies.' Available from https://www.autismassistancedogsireland.ie/case-studies [accessed 6 October 2021].

Barnardos (2018). *Protecting Children: A Child Protection Guide for Early Years and School Age Childcare Services.* Dublin: Barnardos.

Barnardos (2016). *The Key Person Approach: Positive Relationships with Children in the Early Years.* Dublin: Barnardos.

Barnardos (2012). *Child Links: Children with Additional Needs in Early Years Services*. Dublin: Barnardos.

Better Start (n.d.). *National Early Years Quality Development*. Available from https://www.betterstart.ie/

Buckley, S., Bird, G., Sacks, B. and Archer, T. (2006). 'A comparison of mainstream and special education for teenagers with Down syndrome: Implications for parents and teachers.' *Down Syndrome Research and Practice*, 9(3), pp 54–67.

Building Regulations Part M (2012). Available from https://www.irishstatutebook.ie/eli/2010/si/513/made/en/print [accessed 27 August 2021].

Carr-Fanning, Kate. (30 September 2020). *Irish Medical Times*. Available from https://www.imt.ie/clinical/understanding-adhd-impact-30-09-2020/ [accessed 25 August 2021].

Central Statistics Office (CSO) Ireland (2017). 'Census of Population 2017 and families'. Central Statistics Office website.

Central Statistics Office (CSO) Ireland (2019). 'Vital Statistics Yearly Summary 2019'. Available from https://www.cso.ie/en/index.html [accessed 19 August 2021].

Centre for Early Childhood Development and Education (2006) *Síolta: The National Framework for Early Childhood Education*. Dublin: CECDE Available from https://siolta.ie/access_manuals.php [accessed 12 September 2021].

Centre for Early Childhood Development and Education (2006). *Síolta: Síolta Handbook*. Dublin: CECDE. Available from https://siolta.ie/media/pdfs/final_handbook.pdf [accessed 12 September 2021].

Centre for Early Childhood Development and Education (2006) *Síolta: Síolta Research Digest Standard 3 Parents and Families*. Available from https://siolta.ie/media/pdfs/Research%20Digest%20-%20Parents%20and%20Family.pdf [accessed 12 September 2021].

Centre for Early Childhood Development and Education (2006) *Síolta: Síolta Research Digest Standard 11 Professional Practice*. Available from https://siolta.ie/media/pdfs/Research%20Digest%20-%20Professional%20Practice.pdf [accessed 12 September 2021].

Centre for Early Childhood Development and Education (2006) *Síolta: Síolta Research Digest Standard 12 Communication*. Available from https://siolta.ie/media/pdfs/Research%20Djgest%20-%20 Communication.pdf [accessed 12 September 2021].

Child Care Act, 1991. https://www.irishstatutebook.ie/eli/1991/act/17/enacted/en/html [accessed 25 August 2021].

Child Care Act, 1991 (Early Years Services Regulations) 2016. Available from https://www. irishstatutebook.ie/eli/2016/si/221/made/en/print [accessed 28 August 2021].

Children Act, 2001. https://www.irishstatutebook.ie/eli/2001/act/24/enacted/en/html [accessed 25 August 2021].

Dare, A. & O' Donovan, M. (2002). Good Practice in Caring for Young Children with Special Needs. London: Nelson Thornes.

Deer, B. (2011). 'How the case against the MMR vaccine was fixed.' *British Medical Journal*, 342. DOI: https://doi.org/10.1136/bmj.c5347 (Published 06 January 2011)

Department of Children, Equality, Disability, Integration and Youth (2016). *Child Care Act 1991. (Early Years Services) Regulations 2016*. Dublin: Stationery Office.

Department of Children, Equality, Disability, Integration and Youth (2021). *First 5 – A Government Strategy for Babies, Children and Their families 2019–2028*. Available from https://first5.gov.ie/ [accessed 15 September 2021].

Department of Children and Youth Affairs (2016). *Diversity, Equality and Inclusion Charter and Guidelines for Early Childhood Care and Education*. Available from https://assets.gov.ie/38186/ c9e90d89d94b41d3bf00201c98b2ef6a.pdf [accessed 15 September 2021].

Department of Children and Youth Affairs (2017). *Children First: National Guidance for the Protection and Welfare of Children*. Dublin: Stationery Office. Available from https://www.tusla.ie/uploads/ content/Children_First_National_Guidance_2017.pdf [accessed 15 September 2021].

Disability Act, 2005. https://www.irishstatutebook.ie/eli/2005/act/14/enacted/en/html [accessed 24 August 2021].

Diversity, Equality and Inclusion Charter, 2016. Available from https://assets.gov.ie/38186/ c9e90d89d94b41d3bf00201c98b2ef6a.pdf [accessed 28 August 2021].

Donohoe, J. & Gaynor, F. (2011). *Education and Care in the Early Years, 4th ed*. Dublin: Gill & Macmillan.

Donohoe, J., McDermott, E., & Regan, C. (2021). *Professional Practice in ELC*. Tipperary: Boru Press.

Down Syndrome Ireland (n.d.). Local Services and Supports. Available from https://downsyndrome. ie/local-services-and-supports/ [accessed 6 October 2021].

Early Childhood Ireland. (2016). AIM (Access and Inclusion Model). Available from https://www. earlychildhoodireland.ie/?s=AIM [accessed 27 August 2021].

Education Act, 1998. https://www.irishstatutebook.ie/eli/1998/act/51/enacted/en/html [accessed 25 August 2021].

Education for Persons with Special Educational Needs Act 2004. Available from https://www.irishstatutebook.ie/eli/2004/act/30/enacted/en/html [accessed 26 August 2021].

Equal Status Act 2000, 2018. https://www.ihrec.ie/app/uploads/2020/10/IHREC-Equal-Status-Rights-Leaflet-WEB.pdf [accessed 29 August 2021].

First 5 (2019). https://assets.gov.ie/31184/62acc54f4bdf4405b74e53a4afb8e71b.pdf [accessed 29 August 2021].

Flood, E. (2021). *Growth & Development in Early Childhood*. Tipperary: Boru Press.

Flood, E. (2013). *Assisting Children with Special Needs: An Irish Perspective 2nd ed.* Dublin: Gill & Macmillan.

Flood, E., & Hardy, C. (2013). *Early Care & Education Practice*. Dublin: Gill & Macmillan.

Framework for Early Childhood Education. Dublin (2006): Centre for Early Childhood Development and Education.

Fried, P. A. and Smith, A. M. (2001). 'A literature review of the consequences of prenatal marihuana exposure: an emerging theme of a deficiency in aspects of executive function.' *Neurotoxicology and Teratology*, 23(1), pp 1–11.

Gibbs, G. (1988). 'Reflective Cycle.' Available from https://www.toolshero.com/management/gibbs-reflective-cycle-graham-gibbs/ [accessed 1 October 2021].

Glover, V., Mulder, E. J., Van den Bergh, B. R., & Mennes, M. (2005). 'Antenatal maternal anxiety and stress and the neurobehavioural development of the fetus and child: links and possible mechanisms. A review.' *Neuroscience & Biobehavioral Reviews*, 29(2), pp 237–258.

Gray, C. (n.d.). *Social Stories*. Available from Social Stories - Carol Gray - Social Stories (carolgraysocialstories.com) [accessed 2 October 2021].

Health Service Executive (HSE) Ireland, 2021. https://www.hse.ie/eng/ [accessed 24 August 2021].

Health Service Executive (HSE) Ireland. (2021). 'About Asthma.' Available from https://www.hse.ie/eng/. [accessed 19 August 2021].

Johnson, A., (2002). 'Prevalence and characteristics of children with cerebral palsy in Europe.' *Developmental Medicine and Child Neurology*, 44(9), pp 633–640.

Klein, M. D., Cook, R. E., & Richardson-Gibbs, A. M. (2001). *Strategies for Including Children with Special Needs in Early Childhood Settings*. US: Thomson Learning.

Kolb, D. (1984). *Experiential Learning Cycle*. Available from https://www.simplypsychology.org/learning-kolb.html [accessed 1 October 2021].

Law, J., Boyle, J., Harris, F., Harkness, A. & Nye, C. (2000). 'Prevalence and natural history of primary speech and language delay: findings from a systematic review of the literature.' *International Journal of Language and Communication Disorders*, 35, pp 165–188.

227

Longford Childcare Committee (2017). 'Professional Practice in the Early Years.' Available from https://longfordchildcare.ie/professional-practice-early-years/ [accessed 11 October 2021].

Lyons, I. M., Ansari, D. and Beilock, S. L. (2012). 'Symbolic Estrangement: Evidence against a strong association between numerical symbols and the quantities they represent.' *Journal of Experimental Psychology: General*, 141(4), p. 635.

MacLeod-Brudenell, I. (2004). *Advanced Early Years Care and Education*. Oxford: Heinemann.

Marbina, L., Church, A., & Tayler, C. (n.d.). 'Victorian Early Years Learning & Development Framework: Evidence Paper Practice Principle 8; Reflective Practice.' Available from https://www.education.vic.gov.au/Documents/childhood/providers/edcare/evirefprac.pdf [accessed 1 October 2021].

Meggitt, C., Manning-Morton, J., & Bruce, T. (2016). *Childcare and Education 6th ed*.) London: Hodder Education.

My Support Networks (n.d.) *A to Z of Illnesses and Disabilities*. Available from https://mysupportnetwork.ie [accessed 10 October 2021].

National Council for Special Education (2011). *Inclusive Education Framework*. Meath: National Council For Special Education. Available from https://ncse.ie/wp-content/uploads/2014/10/InclusiveEducationFramework_1.pdf [accessed 20 September 2021].

National Curriculum for Assessment (2009). *Aistear: The Early Childhood Curriculum Framework: Guidelines for Good Practice*. Dublin: NCCA. Available from https://ncca.ie/media/4151/aistear_theearlychildhoodcurriculumframework.pdf [accessed 15 September 2021].

National Curriculum for Assessment (2009). *Aistear: The Early Childhood Curriculum Framework: Principles and Themes*. Dublin: NCCA. Available from https://www.curriculumonline.ie/getmedia/484bcc30-28cf-4b24-90c8-502a868bb53a/Aistear-Principles-and-Themes_EN.pdf [accessed 15 September 2021].

National Curriculum for Assessment (2015). *Aistear Síolta Practice Guide*. Available from https://www.aistearsiolta.ie/en/ [accessed 15 September 2021].

NCBI (2021). https://www.ncbi.ie/. [accessed 20 August 2021].

NCSE (2011). *The Education of Deaf and Hard of Hearing Children in Ireland*. Trim: NCSE.

Nicholson, A. (2016). *Recognition and Management of Shaken Baby Syndrome*. Irish Medical Journal.

O'Dea, Á., Stanley, M., Coote, S. Robinson, K. and Dyspraxia Ireland (2021). 'Children and young people's experiences of living with developmental coordination disorder/dyspraxia: A systematic review and meta-ethnography of qualitative research.' *PloS one*, 16(3), p.e0245738.

Quigley, U., Moloney, M., & McCarthy, E. (n.d.). *What Difference: Working effectively with children who have special needs in early years setting*. Limerick: Limerick City Childcare Committee & Mary Immaculate College Curriculum Development Unit.

Rodd, J. (1998). *Leadership in Early Childhood 2nd ed*. Berkshire: Open University Press.

Schon, D. (1983). 'Reflective Model.' Available from: https://nursinganswers.net/reflective-guides/schon-reflective-model.php [accessed 1 October 2021].

Spohr, H. L. & Steinhausen, H. C., 2008. 'Fetal alcohol spectrum disorders and their persisting sequelae in adult life.' *Deutsches Ärzteblatt International*, 105(41), p. 693.

Swan, D. (2000). 'From Exclusion to Inclusion.' *Frontline Magazine.*

Tusla (2017). *Quality and Regulatory Framework: Full Day Care Service and Part-Time Day Care Service.* Dublin: Early Years Inspectorate. Available at https://www.tusla.ie/services/preschool-services/early-years-quality-and-regulatory-framework/ [accessed 20 September 2021].

The United Nations Convention on the Rights of the Child, 1989. Available from https://www.childrensrights.ie/sites/default/files/UNCRCEnglish.pdf [accessed 29 August 2021].

Universal Convention on the Rights of Persons with Disabilities, 2006. Available from https://www.un.org/development/desa/disabilities/convention-on-the-rights-of-persons-with-disabilities/convention-on-the-rights-of-persons-with-disabilities-2.html [accessed 26 August 2021].

Van Meurs, K. (1999). 'Cigarette smoking, pregnancy and the developing fetus.' *Stanford med rev*, 1(1), pp 14–6.

INDEX